ISLAMIC FUNDAMENTALISM, FEMINISM, AND GENDER INEQUALITY IN IRAN UNDER KHOMEINI

Masoud Kazemzadeh

D1563545

University Press of America,® Inc.
Lanham · New York · Oxford

Copyright © 2002 by
University Press of America,® Inc.
4720 Boston Way
Lanham, Maryland 20706

PO Box 317
Oxford
OX2 9RU, UK

ISBN 0-7618-2388-3 (paperback : alk. ppr.)

⊖™ The paper used in this publication meets the minimum
requirements of American National Standard for Information
Sciences—Permanence of Paper for Printed Library Materials,
ANSI Z39.48—1984

This book is dedicated to Dr. Mohammad Mossadegh,
U.S. Supreme Court Justice William Brennan, Jr., and
Parvaneh Eskandari-Forouhar
for their courage and determination in promoting
individual liberties, democracy, and social justice.

CONTENTS

FIGURES

PREFACE AND

ACKNOWLEDGMENTS

In the past two decades we have witnessed the exponential growth of movements throughout the Middle East and North Africa which have claimed allegiance to Islam as their guide to a total transformation of their polities. These militant fundamentalist movements have put the change of women's roles at the very top of their political, social and cultural agendas.

In Afghanistan, the Taliban had forced women to wear the veil, and had forced women out of schools and workplaces. In Egypt and Algeria, militant fundamentalists have specifically targeted women who refuse to wear the veil.

The rise of Islamic fundamentalist movements in the region and their emphasis, indeed obsession, on women's role has given rise to the question of the relationship between Islam and women's inferior position in Islamic polities. Is Islam, as a religion, against the equality of men and women? Is Islamism, that is Islam as a political ideology, against the equality of women? Is Islam as a civilization—that is all groups and individuals regardless of religiosity and ideology in a particular civilization—against the equality of women?

In this book I will analyze the relationship between Islam and gender inequality. I will focus on the case of Iran in my analysis. There are many reasons why I have chosen to focus on Iran as my test case. There are 55 countries which are members of the Organization of the Islamic Conference. Obviously, studying all 55 countries is the most comprehensive research design and one which has many advantages. However, by analyzing one country instead of all the 55, or only several, the analyst chooses depth over breadth. In addition, in each country there are many groups and ideologies; comparing and contrasting these competing groups and ideologies within a single country leads to significant findings. For these reasons, I decided to study only one country.

I have chosen the case of Iran—instead of another country—for several reasons. First, Iran is the first country that the fundamentalists came to power. Second, since June 1981 the fundamentalists have ruled Iran solely by themselves.

Third, and perhaps the most important, is that the Iranian revolution of 1979 was a broad-based coalition against the Shah which included many political groups. From February 1979 until June 1981, when fundamentalists and non-fundamentalists were struggling against each other, Iran enjoyed relative political freedom which allowed space for various groups to articulate different ideas and organize substantial number of people in various organizations.

This unparalleled freedom gave rise to a "laboratory" situation which is relatively absent in other countries. For these reasons I have relied upon Iran in the period between February 1979 and June 1981 as the case to study the relationship between Islam and gender inequality.

This book is primarily written for undergraduate courses in Middle Eastern studies, women's studies, and third world politics.

Although scholars will find ideas and explanations that are original and provocative, I have attempted to describe all the concepts and theories in ways that are comprehensible to the undergraduates. I have included a Glossary, which provides further help. No prior knowledge on Islam, feminism or political science is necessary in order to fully comprehend the finding of this book.

I would like to thank my students in "Introduction to Middle East Politics" for their demand that I put down in words, my answers to their probing questions on this subject. They will find their questions in the following pages. I hope that I have been able to enhance their understanding of this burning and volatile subject.

I would like to thank my own professors whose teachings have influenced the content of this book. They are Mark Kann, Nora Hamilton, Carol Thompson, Judith Stiehm, Eliz Sanasarian, Terrence Ball, and Laurie Brand. They will find their lectures pop up in the following pages and I hope they forgive me for not footnoting their words. I also thank my colleague Valentine Moghadam, who read the manuscript and made numerous corrections. I thank JD Davidson, my Dean at UVSC, and Oscar Jesperson, my department chair, for providing travel grants for research. I am solely responsible for any errors of fact or interpretation in this book.

Finally, I invite readers to criticize and correct the shortcomings of this book including any errors of fact or analysis. It is only through dialogue and criticism that scholarly enterprise moves forward and our knowledge increases. This book is not intended to be the final word on the relationship between Islam, Islamic fundamentalism and gender inequality. It is an introductory first step. I hope that both those who agree and disagree with my interpretation to put forth their arguments. This book deals with an extremely significant issue whose sensitivity only enhances the need for dialogue and understanding.

CHAPTER 1

INTRODUCTION

There is little doubt that Iranian women have been one of the major losers of the 1979 Iranian revolution. Is Islam to blame for the fate of women in revolutionary Iran? Is Islam invariably against gender equality? Is Islamic fundamentalism against gender equality? In other words what is the relationship between Islam and women's inferior position in Muslim societies in general and in revolutionary Iran in particular. In social scientific language, considering the patriarchal rules and relations in revolutionary Iran as the dependent variable, is Islam the independent variable (the causal factor)? In this book I analyze the relationship between Islam and gender inequality in revolutionary Iran.

DEFINITIONS OF "CAUSALITY" AND "ISLAMISM"

Causality can be defined in four ways: a necessary condition, a sufficient condition, a necessary and sufficient condition, and a contributing factor.[1] A necessary condition of causality refers to conditions in which the effect cannot be observed without the hypothesized factor (cause) being present. For example, the presence of oxygen is a necessary condition for the burning of materials such as wood and paper. No oxygen, no fire. We cannot observe fire without the presence of oxygen. If one could observe the dependent variable where the hypothesized factor is not present, one could conclude that the hypothesized factor is not a necessary condition.

Sufficient condition refers to a situation in which anytime we have the hypothesized factor, we should always observe the dependent factor following. For example, the flow of electricity through a wire made of aluminum or copper is sufficient condition for generating heat. Anytime we apply electrical current through such a wire we will observe heat. If we observe the existence of the hypothesized factor where the dependent variable is absent, we could conclude that the hypothesized factor is not a sufficient condition.

Necessary and sufficient condition is the strongest form of causality. If we observe such a relationship between two variables we could confidently say that one causes the other.

A contributing factor is a weak relationship. The effect (or the dependent variable) is observed without the presence of the hypothesized factor, and even where the hypothesized factor is present we may not observe the effect (the dependent variable). A contributing factor simply increases the chances of the effect being observed. For example, smoking cigarette is a contributing factor in causing cancer. In other words, smoking cigarettes is neither the necessary cause, nor a sufficient cause of cancer; however, smoking cigarettes increases the likelihood of cancer.

In this book, I use the term "Islamist" to refer to any individual, group, organization or movement which clearly and self-consciously adopts Islam as its ideology for political action. In Iran, terms "Islamist" and "Islamism" include: (1) fundamentalists such as Khomeini; (2) liberal Islamist, such as Nehzat Azadi (founded by Mehdi Bazargan) and Bani-Sadr, who served as the first elected President; and (3) the People's Mojahedin Organization of Iran (PMOI) which combines Islam and communism. The liberal Islamists and the PMOI advocate a separation of mosque and government; they do not advocate that the clergy should assume top government positions. In other words, they advocate a separation of mosque and state but not a separation of religion and politics. In Iran, only the fundamentalists advocate direct clerical rule. The traditional clerics who advocate political quietism by the clergy and concentrate on purely religious activities are not called "Islamist." I use terms such as "traditional" or "orthodox" to refer to them.

I use the term "secular" to refer to those who advocate separation of religion and politics. A secular individual or group may be devout Muslim, non-practicing Muslim, agnostic or atheist. For secular forces, religion is a private matter. Secular forces and the traditional clerics oppose the turning of Islam into political ideology by the Islamists.

Islamists have explicitly turned Islam into their political ideology.

SCHOLARLY PERSPECTIVES ON THE RELATIONSHIP BETWEEN ISLAM AND THE GENDER POLICIES OF KHOMEINI

There is general agreement that the fundamentalists' misogynistic policies have alienated large numbers of Iranian women. Moreover, the government's reliance on heavy doses of daily coercion to enforce Islamic moral codes has certainly contributed to its unpopularity.[2] Analytically relevant questions are: (1) Is Islam the causal factor? (2) Is Islam as political ideology, Islamism, the causal factor? (3) Is Islamic fundamentalism the causal factor?

Most scholars and many Iranian feminist activists blame these policies as well as the regime's continued use of repression on its Islamic ideology.[3] They argue that the government is headed by a group of devout Muslim fundamentalists; enforcing Islamic moral precepts is part of their belief system. Whether or not it enhances or decreases the government's legitimacy among the population is irrelevant. Due to its ideology, the regime cannot discontinue such policies even if they undermine its longevity. They argue that patriarchal laws are part of the Koran, the Hadith and the Shariah; to assume that an Islamic government (as opposed to a government of Muslim people) would not enforce them is equivalent to asking the Pope to allow abortion or homosexuality.[4] There has emerged a tendency among feminists that it is the Islamic ideology of the regime and its emphasis on the biological and natural inferiority of women which is the cause of much anti-woman legislation in revolutionary Iran.

According to Sanasarian who wrote one of the first studies on Khomeini's gender policies:

> ...for him [Khomeini] the answers to all questions, problems, and conflicts were to be found in Islam. Like any other zealot (in fact, very much like his Christian counterparts of the Middle Ages and the Moral Majority of today), his person and his religion have become one in interpreting Islamic codes. Khomeini's view of the female sex is based on a classic interpretation of the Koran, where the woman is a symbol of disorder, a source of evil, and the cause of **fitna** or seduction. These attributes are inherent in

the nature of the female; therefore, she should cover herself and be governed by the rules and regulations of Islam. In early 1981, in a speech to a group of women, Khomeini declared that 'one of the biggest achievements of the Islamic Revolution was the return of the veil.... If the Islamic Revolution had no other outcome but the veiling of women, this in and of itself is enough for the Revolution.'[5]

According to Haleh Afshar, who is one of the most prominent feminist scholars, Islamic ideology *per se* and other cultural beliefs in Islamic society, such as the notion of "woman as the family honor," are the reason why women have to be supervised, chaperoned and kept under constant surveillance.[6] Under the fundamentalist rule, Afshar argues, the state has assumed the responsibility which was traditionally enforced by the family. Afshar presents a litany of anti-woman legislation and policies such as the closing down of nurseries, the prohibition of full-time work by mothers of young children, and the elimination of the Family Protection Laws of 1967 and 1976 (which restricted male Islamic rights to easy divorce, custody, polygamy, concubines, etc.), policies which she argues are a direct product of Islamic ideology.

According to Shireen Mahdavi, "The position of women in Iran today [under the Islamic Republic] is directly linked to Shi'ism...." After summarizing the views of the leading Shia theologians since the sixteenth century and concluding that they are "identical to that of Khomeini," Mahdavi states: "These interpretations of the Koran have led to woman's unequal position in Iranian society."[7]

Even feminist scholars who set out to challenge the dominant paradigm (which regards Islam as the causal factor in Middle Eastern polities), unwittingly restate the saliency of Islam.[8] Parvin Paidar, for example, in her penetrating study writes: "The rapid Islamisation of women's position pointed once again to the centrality of gender relations in the political ideology of Islam.... Ayatollah Khomeini was adamant that without the Islamic family and women's hejab there could be no Islamic society."[9] As I wrote in a long review of her book:

> Although Paidar begins and ends her book by castigating those who hold an essentialist view of Islam and indeed reiterates this several times in her discussion, her analysis fails to distinguish between fundamentalist and nonfundamentalist clerics and groups. Patriarchy and Islam are treated as one and the same, and the policies of the fundamentalists are treated as though all Islamic groups share that interpretation of Islam. The term

fundamentalism is not even used once in this lengthy book, nor is any other term used to connote a major difference between Khomeini and his supporters, on the one hand, and other Islamic groups, on the other.[10]

There has emerged a number of scholars who have challenged the dominant explanation. Among these one may cite Afsaneh Najmabadi and Valentine Moghadam. Afsaneh Najmabadi in a recent essay criticized her own earlier view of the relationship between Islam and the practice and ideology of the fundamentalist regime. In Najmabadi's own words:

In the literature on Islam and Islamic positions on women, in sources both sympathetic and hostile, including some of my own writings, there is a tendency toward an essentialist conception of Islam, reducing Islam to a given set of doctrines, with a given set of edicts on women, and attributing the current practices and ideology of Islamic movements to the implementation of these doctrines.[11]

In an influential study Moghadam—one of the most influential and prolific feminist scholars—has stated that, "It is my contention that the position of women in the Middle East cannot be attributed to the presumed intrinsic properties of Islam. It is also my position that Islam is neither more nor less patriarchal than other major religions, especially Hinduism and the other two Abrahamic religions, Judaism and Christianity, all of which share the view of women as wife and mother."[12] For Moghadam, "the low status of women and girls is a function not of the intrinsic properties of any one religion but of kin-ordered patriarchal and agrarian structures."[13]

The explanation in the dominant paradigm assigns causal factor significance to Islam as the independent variable causing the misogynist policies implemented in revolutionary Iran. In these studies, scholars simply have assumed and asserted that Islam or Khomeini's ideology has been the causal factor. None has exclusively probed the relationship between these factors.

In this book I analyze the relationship between Islam and the gender policies of Khomeini. Moreover, I attempt to challenge the dominant perspective which has assumed a causal relationship between Islam and Khomeini's misogynist policies. In this book, I attempt to demonstrate that Islam is neither a necessary condition, nor a sufficient condition for gender inequality. The relationship between Islam and gender inequality may be conceptualized as a contributing factor. Islam could be a medium through which gender inequality, or anti-feminism, is expressed. In other words, in Islamic countries, patriarchal groups could use Islam to justify their positions and undermine their opponents.

I believe that the structuralist versus idealist debate on the relationship between Islam and gender inequality is inadequate in fully explaining the relationship. Structuralists insist that socially constructed hierarchies (such as socioeconomic class, patriarchal interests, ethnic groups) which produce and distribute resources and services determine the superstructure (e.g., the laws, religion, gender relations). Idealists insist that the opposite is the case. For the idealists, superstructural factors such as beliefs, values, religion, and culture determine the economy, gender relations and ethnic disparities in power and resources. In this book I demonstrate that the relationship is not uni-directional but dialectical (i.e., bi-directional). Structural factors in the Islamic world have given rise to both misogynist and feminist groups. Islam, as a religion, is a variegated belief system which includes both egalitarian and discriminatory ethos, principles and laws. The misogynist groups pick and choose from Islam those parts which serve their interests and ignore those parts which hamper their interests.

On the one hand, an idealist explanation which locates the source and cause of gender inequality in the Middle East in Islam is wrong. On the other hand, a structuralist explanation which ignores the influence of superstructural factors is also overstating its case. It is my contention that Islam is a contributing factor in the relationship between Islam and gender inequality.

SUMMARY OF THE BOOK

In chapter Two I will discuss in considerable detail Islamic fundamentalist policies and politics regarding women. This is the dependent variable in this study. In chapter Three I will present a discussion of various theories of gender in order to demonstrate that Islamic fundamentalism shares anti-feminism with many other religions and ideologies. In other words, neither Islamic fundamentalism nor Islam is a necessary condition for a gender-unequal polity. Then I proceed to show that there were Islamist and secular political parties in Iran that advocated gender equality. In so doing I will demonstrate that Islam is not a sufficient condition for gender inequality.

Demonstrating that Islam is a contributing factor is a much harder task. To make my argument, in chapter Four I analyze the Koran and illustrate that many verses in the Koran explicitly and expressly assign an inferior position to women. In other words, although many devout Muslims, secular Muslims and non-fundamentalist Islamist political parties are indeed feminist, the Koran itself contains verses which both feminists and anti-feminists could cite for their cause. In chapter Five, I demonstrate that Islamic fundamentalism as it takes form in Iran is a radical departure from Islam and traditional Shiism. In order to do so I contrast the sexual puritanism of the Shia fundamentalists of Iran with the non-puritanism of the Prophet Muhammad and the Shia Imams. One may easily observe that the puritanism of contemporary Islamic fundamentalists has more in common with the puritanism of contemporary Christian fundamentalists and Jewish fundamentalists than with the ethos of original Islam. Again, I intend to demonstrate that Islamic fundamentalists pick and choose which parts of Islam to adopt and which parts to ignore—a tendency which is also shared by Christian fundamentalists and Jewish fundamentalists. Chapter Six concludes this book by summarizing the findings and touching upon a few ramifications of this study.

CHAPTER 2

FUNDAMENTALIST POLICIES
ON GENDER

In a broad-based coalition that included secular liberal democrats, liberal Islamists, Islamic fundamentalists, and communists, the Iranian people succeeded in overthrowing the monarchy on February 11, 1979 in a struggle which lasted about two years. Less than a month after assuming power, Ayatollah Khomeini enraged a large number of women by declaring that all women had to wear the Islamic chador.[1] Khomeini's decree came two days prior to March 8, International Women's Day.

Planned rallies and spontaneous marches were attacked by pro-Khomeini religious zealot shock-troops. This was the first truly popular opposition to both Khomeini and the fundamentalists from within the anti-Shah revolutionary movement.[2] The slogans of the marchers were: "Women's Emancipation Day is Global: it is neither Eastern, nor Western," "Women and Men Became Martyrs: Both Have to Be Free," and "We Condemn Dictatorship in Any Guise."[3] Three days of pitched battles ensued between women and their male supporters on the one hand and pro-Khomeini attackers on the other.[4]

Prime Minister Bazargan, a liberal Islamist, and Ayatollah Taleghani, a popular progressive cleric, "clarified" Khomeini's decree by stating that Khomeini did not mean that all women had to wear the veil, only those who regarded themselves as devout Muslims.[5] The communist Islamist PMOI (which combines a Stalinist interpretation of communism with Islam), condemned the feminist women fighting against Khomeini's order, as suffering from "imperialist culture" and declared "hejab" to be "a revolutionary foundation of Islam."[6]

Despite Khomeini's initial retreat, the fundamentalist forces were able to outmaneuver their rivals both inside and outside the government. The fundamentalists consolidated their control of the governmental apparatus by June 1981 and through a reign of terror decimated their opponents. The process of fundamentalist consolidation involved a continuous struggle partially centered on women's issues; the unrelenting misogynistic policies of the fundamentalists and the resistance they generated colored the immediate post-revolutionary struggles.[7]

Among the most celebrated milestones in post-revolutionary feminist struggles are the protest against Khomeini's order for the dismissal of all female judges,[8] the December 1979 "Women's Conference" and the July 5, 1980, anti-veil demonstrations.[9] The slogans in the 1980 demonstration included: "We did not Participate in the Revolution to Move Backward," "Men and Women are Equal, for they were Both Martyred," and "Iranian Women do not Stay in Chains."[10] With the successful suppression of all open opposition, women seem to have opted for passive resistance to the policies of the fundamentalist elites. For instance, according to the UN Special Commission on Human Rights, in a 12-month period in 1991-92, over 113,000 people (mostly women) were arrested for "moral corruption" and "insufficient veiling."[11]

Before discussing the specific gender policies which Khomeini and the fundamentalists forced upon the Iranian people, it is imperative to present the historical, cultural and political contexts because an identically-worded decree may have totally different meanings in different polities.

HISTORICAL CONTEXT

The Arabian peninsula's major contributions are Islam and the Koran. Iranians, on the other hand, can point to a plethora of cultural and religious achievements. Zoroastrianism and its holy book, the Avesta, are the inventions of Persians and predate not only Islam, but also Christianity and Judaism. Indeed, its monotheism and stories of Heaven and Hell predate Judaism and many of its myths have found their way into Jewish theology, probably incorporated into Judaism by rabbis during the Jewish exile in Babylon before they were freed by Cyrus, the Zoroastrian Persian King.[12]

Although the Prophet Mohammad and his successors Abu Bakr and Omar used the sword to consolidate their power, nevertheless for most of the Arabs of the Arabian peninsula Islam was (and is) a genuine home-grown religion and worldview. On the contrary, Islam was violently imposed on the reluctant and conquered Iranians. In the bloody wars of 637-643 AD (Islamic years 15-23), the Arab-Islamic invaders defeated Iranians, killed hundreds of thousands of Iranians, took as war booty thousands upon thousands of Iranian women and young girls and distrib-uted them among their soldiers and sold them in the slave and concubine bazaars of Mecca and Medina, burned libraries in Iran, and made Iranians second-class subjects in their own homeland forced to pay heavy taxes. The fact that Iranians mounted a protracted war is quite significant considering that the Arab invasion occurred in the wake of a particularly painful period of Iranian history.

The Iranians were forced to accept Islam in order to escape persecution. Even as Muslims the Iranians were treated as second-class Muslims by their less literate Arab conquerors. The Iranians adopted Sunni Islam and were Sunnis until the Safavid dynasty established itself in northwestern Iran (today's Azerbaijan province) and literally through the sword converted hitherto Sunni Iranians to the Shia denomination of Islam beginning in 1501. The only Iranians who are Sunni today are those who lived on the periphery of the Iranian heartland, too far away to have been subdued by the Safavid kings (i.e., Baluchis, Turkoman, and half the Kurdish popula-tion living either in the mountainous region or located in places that came under the rule of the Ottoman Empire at one time or another).

In sum, for the people of the Arabian Peninsula Islam is a genuine reflection of their values and mores. In Iran, Islam is the ideology of the invading foreign colonizers. Both Iranian nationalism and culture are in constant tension with Islam (in both Shia and Sunni versions). The Arab-Islamic conquest of Iran was in effect the cultural genocide of Iranians: Iranians lost their independence, sovereignty, culture, alphabet, religion, and mores.

CULTURAL CONTEXT

Iranians can and do rely upon many sources of cultural identity which are not Islamic. For example, Ferdowsi's *Shahname*, which is widely regarded to be equal to, if not superior to, Homer's *Iliad*, is memorized and recited by literate and illiterate Iranians alike. The works of Omar Khayyam, Hafez and Saadi are cultural icons for the Iranians. Iran has a long history of scientific achievement unequaled in the Arabian peninsula. For example, Razi (865-925 A.D.) known in the West as Rhazes, and Ibn Sina (980-1037 A.D.), known in the west as Avecina, made major scientific contributions to world civilization. Razi compiled the first medical encyclopedia in history (more than twenty volumes). Ibn Sina recognized the contagious nature of some diseases. Ibn Sina's *Canon of Medicine* (al-Kanun) "was the chief medical book of the Middle East and Western Europe from the twelfth to the seventeenth century."[13] Ferdowsi, Khayyam, Hafez, Saadi and Razi were declared a *mortad* (one who commits blasphemy and therefore, should be killed) by their contemporary Islamic clerics.

After coming to power, the fundamentalists started a massive attack on "Iranian identity" and attempted to replace it with an "Islamic identity" for the people in Iran. For the fundamentalists, "ommat Islami" [Islamic community] is the only true source of identity and nationalist allegiance is false and anti-Islamic. In a recent interview on the reason why the fundamentalist leaders attacked Iranian identity, one of the experts from the fundamentalist regime said: "...some of the fundamentalist leaders believed that by accepting the genuineness of Iranian identity and giving legitimacy to Iranian civilization, it was possible to undermine and hurt the legitimacy and credibility of the Islamic identity."[14] Since the Iranian revolution, fundamentalist leaders have deemphasized, banned, or maligned these icons of Iranian civilization in the state media and school textbooks.[15] Ayatollah Sadeq Khalkhali, the infamous "hanging judge" who was one of the closest associates of Khomeini organized a group to bulldoze Ferdowsi's tomb in Tus near Mashhad. Only the intervention by then-Prime Minister Mehdi Bazargan and his entire cabinet (which was composed of liberal Islamists and secular liberal democrats) prevented Khalkhali from carrying out this plan. The fundamentalist assault on "Iranian identity" and their attempt to replace it with "Islamic identity" backfired within one generation. This has given rise to a "crisis of identity" among young Iranians who have in large numbers abandoned Islamic identity and have embraced Iranian identity more than any time in Iran's recent history.

POLITICAL CONTEXT ONE
TWENTIETH CENTURY POLITICAL STRUGGLES IN IRAN

With the partial exception of Turkey and Egypt, Iran's political development is more advanced than any other country in the Middle East. Iran went through a successful constitutional revolution in 1905-11, where a liberal democratic constitution and a bill of rights were established. Ever since 1907 Iran has had a parliament, although the elections have infrequently been open and free.

After World War Two, Iran experienced genuine democracy with free multi-party elections and a free press. Labor unions were organized by socialists, communists and trade unionists in much of Iran.[16] Dr. Mossadegh, a popular secular liberal democrat, was freely elected and his Iran National Front carried the nationalization of Iranian oil and pressured the Shah to respect the constitutional restrictions on his power. It was direct intervention by the CIA and the British secret service MI6 that overthrew Dr. Mossadegh's democratic government and replaced it with the dictatorial regime of the Shah.

Most political parties continued their struggles against the Shah and demanded the return of democracy. The only major political party which supported the Shah was Iran's pro-Nazi SOMEKA (Socialist and Nationalist Party of the Iranian Nation). The Shah and the CIA rewarded SOMEKA leaders with several important positions. General Fazlollah Zahedi, who had been arrested and imprisoned by the British during the WWII for his coup attempt to establish a pro-Nazi government was made Prime Minister. Mr. Sharif-Emami, who also had spent time in jail for his pro-Nazi activities in the 1940s, held several important positions including head of the Oil Industry, President of the Senate, and Prime Minister. Mr. Bahram Shahrokh, who was a trainee of Joseph Goebbels and Berlin Radio's Farsi program announcer during the Nazi period, became Director of Propaganda. Most scholars believe that had it not been for the American and British intervention, Iran would have remained a secular democracy in the post-World War Two period.[17]

The Iranian revolution of 1979 was carried out by a broad-based coalition against the Shah who was regarded by most Iranians to be a puppet of the U.S. and a fascist.

POLITICAL CONTEXT TWO
A BRIEF HISTORY OF WOMEN'S AND FEMINIST
STRUGGLES IN IRAN

The violent clashes on March 7-10, 1979 between pro-Khomeini shock troops and large numbers of women who publicly opposed Khomeini's decree on Islamic dress code, as well as the subsequent women's struggle demonstrates that this sector of Iranian society did not support Khomeini.[18] This massive rebellion against Khomeini, which was reported worldwide, was the first indication that not all Iranians who struggled against the Shah supported Khomeini's policies.[19] The subsequent women's struggles indicate that the March 1979 rebellion was not an aberration but a turning point in the feminist movement in modern Iran, a movement which goes back to the mid-19th century.

The first Iranian woman to publicly advocate the equality of women and to appear in public without the veil was Qurratulain (born 1820).[20]

Another pioneer, Ms. Sedigheh Dolatabadi, started Iran's first feminist (not merely a woman's) journal and a girls' school. Ms. Dolatabadi was invited to join the (the United States') National Women's Party's "International Advisory Council" and she attended the International Women's Suffrage Alliance held in Paris in 1926.[21]

Dolatabadi and other Iranian feminists were to a large degree the product of the Constitutional movement that gave rise to a militant women's movement.[22] When in December 1911 the Tzarist Russian government gave an ultimatum to the Iranian Majles (parliament):

> About a hundred women took a Persian flag and went into Parliament, saying to the men, 'If you are not going to fight with Russia, we women go to be killed that we may not see our homes ruined.' And the following days they went from tea-shop to tea-shop and broke the cups and the tea-pots. They smashed the windows of shops selling Russian goods, and compelled men to take off their Russian goloshes and to remove Russian collars in the streets. For three weeks they stopped all the tramcars. Many of them are still boycotting Russian goods.[23]

Apparently referring to the same incident, William Morgan Shuster, whose expulsion from Iran was a key Russian demand, writes:

Out from their walled courtyards and harems marched three hundred of the weak sex, with the flush of undying determination in their cheeks. They were clad in their plain black robes with the white nets of their veils dropped over their faces. Many held pistols under their skirts or in the folds of their sleeves. Straight to the Medjlis [Majles] they went, and, gathered there, demanded of the President [Speaker of the Majles] that he admit them all.... In his reception-hall they confronted him [the Speaker of Majles], and lest he and his colleagues should doubt their meaning, these cloistered Persian mothers, wives, and daughters exhibited threateningly their revolvers, tore aside their veils, and confessed their decision to kill their own husbands and sons, and leave behind their own dead bodies, if the deputies wavered in their duty to uphold the liberty and dignity of the Persian people and nation.[24]

Outside the Majles, thousands of women were among the more than fifty thousand people who marched toward the Majles. Several women's *anjoman* (secret committee or association) sponsored the march and the general strike. Many of the women of the Anjoman of Ladies of the Nation "took to the podium, gave passionate speeches in defense of the revolution, and demanded that the Majles resist the ultimatum of foreign powers. The poet Zaynab Amin, a founding member of Anjoman of Ladies of the Nation and a teacher at the Shahabad Girls School, recited some of her poems, which called for the defense of the nation."[25] Morgan Shuster, writing in 1912, says:

The Persian woman since 1907 had become almost at a bound the most progressive, not to say radical, in the world. That this statement upsets the ideas of centuries makes no difference. It is the fact.

During the five years following the successful but bloodless revolution in 1906 against the oppression and cruelty of Muzaffaru'd-Din Shah, a feverish and at times fierce light has shone in the veiled eyes of Persia's women, and in their struggle for liberty and its modern expressions, they broke through some of the most sacred customs which for centuries past have bound their sex in the land of Iran.

...what shall we say of the veiled women of the Near East who overnight become teachers, newspaper writers, founders of women's clubs and speakers on political subjects? What, when we find them vigorously propagating the most progressive ideas of the Occident in a land until recently wrapped in the hush and gloom of centuries of despotism?[26]

According to Shuster, women organized a vigorous movement which, among other things, helped him in his task in aiding the Constitutional government withstand pressures from Russian and British governments and their Iranian (absolutist) monarchist allies. In his words:

> The Persian women have given to the world a notable example of the ability of unsullied minds to assimilate rapidly an absolutely new idea, and with the elan of the crusader who has a vision, they early set to work to accomplish their ideals.
>
> ...It was well known in Teheran that there were dozens of more or less secret societies among Persian women, with a central organization by which they were controlled. To this day I know neither the names nor the faces of the leaders of this group, but in a hundred different ways I learned from time to time that I was being aided and supported by the patriotic fervor of thousands of the weaker sex.[27]

Apparently the feminist demand for education had become so widespread by 1911—despite vigorous and violent opposition of the Islamic clerics—that a four-year-old girl "had received a present of fruit and a proposal of marriage from her cousin, two years older, and she had answered: 'I must first go to school.'"[28]

Ever since the 1906 Constitutional revolution, *Masaleh Zanan* (the Women's Question) has been a prominent issue in Iranian politics. Even under Reza Shah, when the independent women's movement was co-opted and repressed, the 1936 law banning the veil illustrates that the issue of women's role was prominent. And when Reza Shah's regime fell due to the Allied military invasion of Iran in 1941, the Shia clerics (15 of the highest-ranking members of the clergy) issued a joint fatva (religious decree) prohibiting women to appear in bazaar and mosques without the chador.[29] And again Mossadegh's decision to enfranchise women was a major cause of Ayatollah Kashani's break with Mossadegh and Kashani's alliance with Mohammad Reza Shah.[30] And again it was the bill allowing women (and non-Muslims) the right to vote and be elected (along with land reform) that prompted Khomeini—an unknown minor hojatolislam—to criticize the Shah in 1962. In the words of Edward Mortimer:

> ...up to 1959 the Iranian *ulama*, although no longer in control of the country's legal and educational systems, remained a prosperous and influential group of people whom the government treated with respect and who, though generally willing to support the government, could certainly

not be taken for granted. The conflict between them and Muhammad Reza Shah can be dated only from 1959. The first signs of it came in January of that year, when new proposals to enfranchise women were sharply criticized by Bihbihani and others.[31]

At no time in Iranian history has the issue of gender been more salient than in the period after the 1979 revolution. According to Afsaneh Najmabadi, "Women have acquired a very prominent position in the ideology as well as practice of the Islamic Revolution and the Islamic Republic."[32] The fundamentalists included two paragraphs specifically on women in the preface to the Constitution of the Islamic Republic under the subtitle "Woman in the Constitution."[33] All major opposition groups have included specific articles in their constitutions demanding equality of women and the abolition of discriminatory laws that have been promulgated by the Islamic Republic.

THE GENDER POLICIES OF KHOMEINI AND FUNDAMENTALISTS IN IRAN

Now that the historical, cultural and political contexts of Iran have been discussed, we can turn to the specific policies which the fundamentalists pursued in the revolutionary period. The following incident captures the fundamentalists' views on women's rights. In 1991, a major Tehran daily newspaper mentioned that Khomeini's influential son, Hojatolislam Ahmad Khomeini, believed that men and women were equal. In an angry response he refuted the "accusation" and said: "According to the Shariah, women are subordinate to their husband's will, except where the Shariah makes explicit exceptions."[34]

A major concern of the fundamentalists in revolutionary Iran was women. Through *de jure* and *de facto* discriminations, women were forced into second class citizenship. The task of this section is to describe these policies. It is not any one particular law or policy which is analytically important but the cumulative effect of *de jure* and *de facto* discriminations which created the ultra-patriarchal milieu which is important for this study.

As argued by Marilyn Frye, any one policy on women (usually justified on the grounds that women need the protection which that law would provide) may seem like a golden bar viewed in isolation and indeed may provide some protection, but if one looks at the whole picture, one will see that the constellation is nothing but a cage made of golden bars which imprisons women.[35] The description of this "golden cage" is the goal of this section. Prior to describing these policies it is important to issue the following caveats: (1) although these policies are anchored in the Shariah [Islamic law], they constitute only one interpretation of it; and (2) many of these policies were diluted or reversed in the late 1980s and early 1990s after the fundamentalists had consolidated state power and decimated their opponents.

Patriarchal interests and gender issues for Ayatollah Khomeini and the fundamentalists constitute a salient aspect of their politics. Through *de jure* discrimination the fundamentalists enshrined patriarchal interests as the law of the land. The Constitution of the Islamic Republic, for example, assigns the most powerful position, *Velayat Faghih* (Supreme Leader), to a mojtahed (a very high-ranking Islamic cleric who can issue fatva) who, by definition, is male.[36] The second most powerful position is that of the President. Article 115 of the Constitution specifically states that only **males** can become President. The Preamble, after acknowledging the massive participation of women during the uprising against the Shah, extols the family unit and the role of women within it. It states the goal of the Islamic government to be "the removal of women (from being objects) or (becoming a tool of labor) in the service of consumerism and exploitation and regaining the vital and honorable duty of motherhood in rearing religious children."[37] The Constitution established a system which denied **juridical** equality to women.[38]

The Bill of Retribution, or the criminal code, called Qanon Qesas, is probably one of the most misogynistic codes of law in existence in any contemporary society. The entire legal code is premised on the assumption that women are not rational beings and are worth less than men. Article 33, for example, says: "Testimony: a) A case of willful murder is proved only on the basis of two righteous men's testimony; b) a case of semi-willful or unintentional murder is proved on the basis of the testimony of two righteous men, or (the testimony) of one righteous man and two righteous women, or that of one righteous man and the plaintiff's oath."[39] Articles 5, 6 and 46 allow a wealthy Muslim man to kill an indigent Muslim woman and only pay a small amount of money to her guardian, and go free.[40]

The already-patriarchal pre-revolution Civil Code was revised to become even more patriarchal after the 1979 revolution.[41] In the 1991 session, the Majles revised Laws #1043 and #1044 of the Civil Code. According to these laws, a 30-year-old woman who has never been married cannot marry a man without the express permission of her father, paternal

fore-father, or a judge (who is also male).[42] There are no such restrictions
or requirements for males. According to the Civil Code, "Muslim women
are absolutely forbidden from marrying non-Muslim men and are required
to obtain the government's permission to marry a non-Iranian."[43] However,
there are no restrictions on male's marriage partners.

Less than a month after assuming power Ayatollah Khomeini declared
the Family Protection Law (FPL) of 1967 and its revised amendments in
1975 to be null and void.[44] The FPL had restricted the Shariah, which
grants men complete power to repudiate and/or divorce their wives at will
(without having to register it or have it notarized by a court) and restricted
(although not abolished) polygyny. Due to the FPL, a judge in a court of
law had then the power to grant divorce.[45] According to fundamentalists
"...that the power to divorce has been put in the male's hands is among the
most just of all Islamic laws.... If a woman could divorce her husband, it is
possible that due to her moodiness she would fall into a condition which
she would make an irrational decision; this condition [moodiness and
irrationality] does not exist for males."[46]

According to the Shariah, a man may divorce his wife by simply
announcing it to two males. A woman cannot divorce her husband except
under exceptional circumstances and after a religious judge allows her.[47]
Prior to the passage of the 1967 Family Protection Law, Iran had the
world's fourth highest divorce rate (after the U.S., Egypt, and the Soviet
Union).[48] After the passage of the FPL, the number of divorces in the
population decreased dramatically.[49] In three years (in 1970), this rate
reached 0.6 per 1,000 people, which was a reduction of 50% compared to
10 years earlier and 40% less compared to 5 years earlier.[50] Akbar
Aghajanian, an Iranian sociologist-demographer, attributes this decline to
the FPL which limited men's unilateral and unlimited power to divorce
women and required the court's permission for divorce.[51] The Iranian
historian Gholam-Reza Vatandoust concurs; in his words:

Perhaps this sudden decrease in the divorce rate can be attributed to the
fact that men could no longer divorce their wives at will. They were
required to petition for divorce through family courts, which could make
the process cumbersome and irritating. This, added to the fact that
frequently the man, as breadwinner, had to assume the cost of litigation,
pay the *mihr* (dowry), and provide for child custody, often discouraged
men from arbitrary divorce.[52]

The courts would allow a divorce after all attempts at reconciliation had failed. This perhaps is responsible for a huge reduction in the total number of divorces. Prior to the FPL, in 1966, there were 25,000 divorces. In 1970, there were only 16,000. The rate of divorce per marriages also declined from 16.5% in 1966 to 10% in 1970.[53] After the fundamentalists abolished the FPL and returned the male's Shariah right of unilateral and unlimited divorce rights, in 1980, the number and the rate of divorce skyrocketed again. In 1979, there were 15,000 divorces; the next year, in 1980, there were 24,000; and by 1986 it reached 35,000.[54]

Islamic fundamentalists in Iran constantly reiterate the importance of the **family**. The Preamble of the Constitution of the Islamic Republic states: "The family unit is the foundation of society and the main institution for the growth and advancement of mankind." Article 10 of the Constitution declares: "Since the family is the fundamental unit of Islamic society, all pertinent laws, regulations and policies must facilitate the establishment of family and protect its sanctity and stability of family relations on the basis of Islamic laws and ethics."

Khomeini publicly announced that the Family Protection Law of 1967 and the 1975 amendments to it were null and void, thus restoring men's Shariah right of polygyny. There seems to be a disjunction between the stated goal of establishing permanent, stable families and both the Islamic and the fundamentalist justifications of polygyny.

The ulama--both Shia and Sunni--justify polygyny on the grounds that due to wars there are more women than men in society and that allowing men to marry more than one woman would save her from poverty, prostitution and causing "fetneh" (seduction, sedition).[55] In Khomeini's words:

> The law of the four wives is a very progressive law, and was written for the good of women, since there are more women than men. More women are born than men, and more men are killed in war than women. A woman needs a man, so what can we do, since there are more women than men in the world? Would you prefer that the excess number of women became whores—or that they married a man with other wives?[56]

According to census data from the years 1956, 1966, 1976 and 1986 we know that there have been more men than women in Iran (see Figure 2-1).[57] In 1986, for example, according to census data published by the Islamic Republic there were exactly 1,116,912 more men than women in Iran.[58]

Islamic ideology maintains that polygyny is justified and necessary because there are more women than men in any given society. The fact of the matter is that there are more men in Iran than there are women. If we follow the line of argument of Ayatollah Khomeini, we should expect that now because there are more men than women there ought to be polyandry. The policy of allowing polygyny despite the incorrectness of the ideological justification indicates that it is patriarchal privilege as well as class interests which dictate policies, not putative ideological justifications.

Many in the pre-capitalist mode of production, especially those at the upper echelons of it (i.e., the ulama, bazaaris, landowners), tend to engage in polygyny. Despite bad economic conditions in the post-revolution period, government-released data reveal that polygyny is on the rise. In 1976 there were 86,962 women who were in polygynous marriages (women who wedded married men); in 1986, that number increased to 188,137.[59]

It is important to reiterate that a man in Shia Islam many have up to four permanent wives and unlimited temporary wives (sigheh, or mutah) simultaneously. But women can have only one man at a time as either a permanent husband or as a temporary husband.[60] Is the Islamic law that permit multiple wives a reflection of the perceptions of the biology of men and women or is it a derivative of economic and patriarchal privileges?

The practice of polygyny (in all Muslim countries) and temporary marriages (in Shia countries) as aspects of family and gender relations are practices that scholars attribute to Islam and Islamic law in Muslim countries. In other words, Islam is the independent causal variable that explains male/female sexual inequality.

In Latin America, many men frequent prostitutes and those wealthy enough to do so maintain a permanent mistress. Certainly, Catholicism does not condone these practices, which according to official dogma are sins. If both in Islamic and Catholic countries men have more than one sexual partners whereas women are restricted to one, then Islam cannot be the independent variable. An alternative explication using gender and class analyses, for example, may explain how what is called machismo in one society is referred to as males' Islamic privilege in the other.[61]

Most scholars point to Islam as the explanatory (independent) variable; whereas the overwhelming majority of scholars blame Islam for these practices, fundamentalists credit Islam with understanding human nature (i.e., that males are endowed with a different nature than women, that males need more than one partner). If Islamic fundamentalists are correct that it is nature and not patriarchal power that determines Islamic law, then one would not expect that women need to have more than one sexual partner (that is because of their nature). The fact that Shariah prescribes severe punishment for adulterous women (stoning to death) indicates that the power of the state is needed to restrain women. Phenomena that are innate and natural are not in need of reinforcements and proscriptions. The fact that Shariah allows men multiple partners and restricts women to only one is a reflection more of patriarchy than of nature. Certainly, the fundamentalists' biological determinist reasoning overstates their case. Whereas Islam regulates polygyny, Latin American polities look the other way. In other words, Islam is not the necessary condition for *de facto* polygyny. Hence, culture and Islam are intervening variables that do not cause the dependent variable but only shape it.

In the post-revolutionary period, laws and statutes have been passed which bar women from getting a job or even staying at a hotel without the written (and notarized) permission of her husband or father. According to post-revolution laws, hotels cannot admit an unaccompanied woman unless and until the woman procures a special permit from the local police station stating the duration and purpose of her stay.[62] The post-revolution Civil Code #1117 and Article 54 of the Preliminary Labor Law state: "Married women could be employed in positions which would not harm their marriage. If employment would cause a reduction in the rights of the husband, employment may be granted only after the permission and the consent of the husband."[63]

In 1985 the Second Majles (1984-1988) passed a law banning unmarried women from going abroad to study; the law specified that only married women may go abroad to study if, and only if, they are accompanied by their husbands.[64] An attempt to pass an amendment to that law making an exemption for post-graduate women seeking doctoral degrees failed to even reach the floor of the Third Majles (1988-1992).[65] The law notwithstanding, young women continue to get passports and go abroad to pursue university education in all levels. In other words, the executive branch and the people have simply ignored the laws passed by the legislature.

According to the Shia Shariah, a woman cannot become a judge.[66] After the revolution, women judges were dismissed and told to look for secretarial and administrative jobs.[67] Women lawyers were allowed to work, though harassment was the order of the day. For example, according to a female attorney, judges tended to rule against clients if their lawyer was female.[68] Females were discouraged from entering law school.[69]

Dismissal of Employed Urban Women

Some argue that more devastating than *de jure*, was *de facto* discrimination. Immediately after the revolution the fundamentalists pursued policies aimed at the removal of women from the paid labor force. We do not know exactly how many women were fired. Most early studies relied upon anecdotal evidence. The release of statistical data in the post-1985 period allows us to at least estimate the scope of the firings. According to official Iranian government sources, in 1976 nearly 1,200,000 women were employed; in 1986 that number was reduced to about 920,000.[70] This is an absolute reduction of 280,000 females employed. The actual number of women fired is not known because many were fired and some new women were hired to perform certain necessary functions that have traditionally been done by women.[71] However, the real magnitude of the firings can be understood and put into context by considering the following realities: (1) the absolute number of women increased by 7,811,652 in the previous decade from 16,352,397 in 1976 to 24,164,049 in 1986;[72] (2) many women had to be hired to staff female schools along with nurses to tend to war-related injuries; and (3) many female supporters of the fundamentalists were hired to monitor the dress codes of the population and to enforce the "anti-vice" decrees. According to the government's Statistical Centre of Iran, in 1971, women constituted 11% of the employed; this rate increased in the pre-revolution period to 13.8% in 1976; however, in the **post-revolution** era this number **declined** to 8.9% by 1986.[73]

Through a mix of incentives and outright coercion the fundamentalists forced women out of the labor market (especially in urban areas). Early retirement programs were offered to women who had worked as few as 15 years (instead of the usual 30 years) without loss of entitlement. A woman with a working husband was offered the full wife's wage if she resigned. Women in certain occupations (e.g., judgeships and high government positions) were summarily dismissed or offered lower positions. The imposition of hejab led some independent women to resign rather than endure the veil. Many day-care centers at factories and offices were closed to make it harder for mothers to work.[74]

According to Val Moghadam, who is one of the most prolific and sophisticated scholars of Iran, Khomeini's repeated public calls for women to abandon the paid labor force and assume their God-given domestic roles were targeted to urban women. Rural women whose role in agricultural production was indispensable for the economy have never been under attack by the fundamentalists.[75] In this section I will analyze the data gathered in the census of 1976 and 1986. In particular I will analyze the rate of unemployment for urban women and the proportion of employed females as a percentage of the total female population in urban areas. My analysis of the census data comparing these rates in 1976 (two to three years before the revolution) and in 1986 (the first census data after the revolution) reveals significant changes (see Figs. 2-2 and 2-3).

In 1976, the rate of unemployment for women in urban areas was 5.9%; this rate rose to 29.1% in 1986. Some of this increase is certainly due to the terrible economic situation, but that alone cannot explain the whole story. A comparison with the unemployment rate for males in urban areas reveals a marked difference. In 1976, the rate of unemployment for men in urban areas was 5.0%; this rate rose to 13.6% in 1986. In 1976 the rate of unemployment was almost the same for women and men; the difference was only 0.9%. However, by 1986, there was a huge gap of 15.5% between the two rates. If economic circumstances were the sole factor, we should not witness such a huge difference. This difference is probably due to the fundamentalist policies of firing women and employing men when and where job opportunities were available.

It appears that the fundamentalist elite was able to implement Khomeini's stated goal. There are two vantage points from which one may analyze the situation. The first—just presented—looked at the rate of unemployment, i.e., those who are actively looking for a job and are unable to secure one. That statistic, although important, may not always illuminate all the nuances of a situation (e.g., it is conceivable but not probable in our case that there are a large number of under-qualified women looking for jobs or that the proportion of discouraged unemployed men is higher). A second statistic which, in conjunction with the first, would eliminate the lacuna inherent in the first statistic is the percentage of employed females in the total female population who are 10-years-old and above in urban areas. A decrease of such employed females from 1976 to 1986 would indicate that in relative terms (to the population) fewer women had jobs. In other words, despite looking very hard to get employment, fewer women were able to secure it.

In 1976, 8.5% of urban females 10-years-old and older held jobs, in 1986 that figure dropped to 5.9%; this is a relative decrease of 31%.[76] This significant decrease is even more telling when compared with the finding that the employment participation rate for men did not drop as significantly despite the fact that the economy was experiencing terrible difficulties. In

1976, 60.7% of urban males 10-years-old and older were employed; that figure dropped slightly to 57.7%, which is a relative decrease of less than 5%.[77]

One may distinguish three major sectors among the employed urban females: (1) white-collar salaried employees who primarily came from either the traditional middle class or the modern middle class families; (2) blue-collar workers; and (3) modern middle class professionals. Although the fundamentalists seemed most eager to attack modern middle class women, the following analysis seems to indicate that they had the most success in driving the first two groups out of the labor market.

Although more in-depth studies are necessary, preliminary analysis of the available data seems to indicate that the women who are most affected by fundamentalist policies are those with a high school education or less. Apparently, despite conscious fundamentalist policies, women with higher education have been able to hold onto some jobs. In 1971, 14% of women with a higher education were employed. In 1986 [Iranian calendar year 1365], 24% of women with a higher education were employed, which is an increase of 10% over 15 years earlier. However, the total proportion of women working outside the home decreased from 11% in 1971 to 8.6% in 1986.[78] Whereas the rate of employment of women with higher education was only 3 percentage points higher than all women, in the post-revolution period the gap increased to more than 15 points.

Perhaps it has been easier to replace blue-collar and white-collar (salaried employees) women with men than those women with a higher education.[79] In 1976 (before the revolution) women constituted 12.0% of the salaried employees; this rate was reduced to 9.5% in 1986 (after the revolution). The reduction is even more significant among blue-collar workers. In 1976, women constituted 38.4% of the manufacturing employees; this rate was reduced to 14.4% in 1986.[80]

These statistics reveal that while well-educated women (i.e., professional modern middle class) can find work the employment opportunities of blue-collar and white-collar female workers have deteriorated. Women with a high school diploma or with less education have little chance of employment; men with equal education are preferred.[81]

What these statistics do not reveal is the quality of jobs which women with higher education obtain. Although many have been able to become teachers, nurses and physicians, it has not been easy for women to get other jobs which the fundamentalists would like to see filled by males. Anecdotes of discrimination abound; even fundamentalist women's magazines report that women encounter many difficulties in securing employment in their field. The semi-governmental women's weekly *Zan-e Rouz* reported that a female who had a Masters degree in Urban Planning had to become an attendant in a day-care center.[82] She was reportedly told by the government agencies that "they do not want to hire women."[83] Another woman who had an engineering degree in architecture from Italy had to accept a job as an elementary school teacher. In her query of a responsible authority in the Tehran Municipality Office as to why only men were hired, she was told that "it has been determined that ladies should stay at home and tend to the housework."[84]

Limiting Women's Access to Higher Education

In this section I argue that Khomeini's policies reduced women's access to higher education. Before the revolution, female students in higher education (colleges, two-year teachers training colleges, nursing schools and universities) constituted 40% of the student body; in 1983 their share was reduced to only 10%.[85] Considering the fact that there was an absolute decline in the total number of students in universities the attempt to bar women from universities is even more pronounced. For example, the total number of students at Tehran University alone declined from 17,000 in the 1978/79 academic year to 4,500 in 1983/84.[86] Moreover, the segregation of coeducational facilities and the new law requiring female teachers for female students and the increase in demand for nurses due to the war would lead one to speculate that more women in these fields would mean even fewer women in other fields.

The socio-economic development of the Pahlavi era, particularly in the 1970s, led to acute shortages in human capital. To train and educate the work force for this rapidly expanding economy the Shah substantially expanded higher education. The number of women enrolled in higher education increased from under 5,000 in 1966 to over 74,000 in 1977.[87] As part of returning women to their "proper" place at home and concomitantly opening places for men in universities, the fundamentalists pursued discriminatory policies which denied women admission in many fields.

In order to implement their policies, the fundamentalists attacked the universities under the guise of "the Islamic Cultural Revolution" and the "Islamization" of the curriculum, faculty and student body. After a week of bloody struggles between the secular liberals and communists on the one hand and the fundamentalists on the other, the secular forces were defeated.[88] Subsequently the universities were closed for about two years, during which time most of the politically active faculty with liberal democratic, socialist and Marxist leanings were fired or arrested, with many going into self-imposed exile rather than submit to fundamentalist inquisition.

The new "Islamicized" higher education had two major goals: first, to purge anti-fundamentalist students from the student body; and, second, to segregate men and women into different fields and to reduce the number of women in certain fields. In order to implement the first goal a general requirement for all candidates for admission to the university was established. All students had to sign a written document stating these: (1) "Belief in the religion of Islam or one of the recognized religions in the Constitution"; and (2) "that they lack any kind of connection to or sympathy with any organizations, political parties or groups that are anti-government."[89]

After a student passes the *Konkor*, the national university entrance exam, authorities commence an investigation into the political loyalty of the candidate.[90] According to Sahar Ghahreman:

> ...the admission of the candidate is conditional until the 'local investigations' prove that the candidate is politically and ideologically committed to the ruling regime. The investigations are done on the neighbors about the candidate. For women candidates it has to be proven that the prospective student has a history of conforming to the veiling requirement and that she performs the religious duties such as namaz, fasting, etc. In addition, the high school has to notarize that the candidates for university have never been involved in political activities against the [fundamentalist] government.[91]

In order to achieve the second goal, a large number of the fields in higher education were closed to women candidates, and in other fields a ceiling was established for women candidates. Before the revolution, women were excluded from only two majors in higher education, mining and religious studies. After the "Islamization" of the universities, women were prohibited from studying in 91 of the 169 majors offered in Iranian universities and other institutions of higher education.[92] In other words, women were forbidden to take classes in 54% of the majors offered in higher education. In addition, ceiling percentages were established on the maximum number of women who could be admitted to other fields. These ceilings ranged from 10 to 50 percent; in other words, males were guaranteed at least 50 to 90 percent of the seats in majors which did not exclude women.[93]

It is important to note that for every seat available in higher education there are about 10 or 11 candidates. There has been a dramatic reduction in the number of seats available in the post-revolution period. Whereas in 1977 there were more than 74,000 **women** in higher education, by 1991-92 school year there were only 70,000 seats available for **all** candidates. In 1991, there were about 900,000 candidates for those 70,000 seats.[94]

REPRESSION AND RESISTANCE IN POST-REVOLUTIONARY IRAN

After the overthrow of the monarchy an intense struggle ensued among various elements of the revolutionary coalition. Khomeini and his fundamentalist followers were able to undermine liberal Islamists (Prime Minister Bazargan and President Bani Sadr), secular liberal democrats of the Iran National Front, communist Islamists (PMOI), high-ranking Shia clerics and the communists. The fundamentalists succeeded in consolidating power through massive repression and created one of the most reactionary and oppressive regimes in the world since World War II. Although the fundamentalists were "equal opportunity" repressors and meted out swift executions to their opponents regardless of gender, ethnicity, class, religion, and religiosity, nevertheless women took the brunt of fundamentalist repression.

General Repression

During the First Reign of Terror, from June 21, 1981 until December 1982, somewhere between 12,000 and 20,000 political opponents were executed.[95] During the Second Reign of Terror, from mid-1988 to mid-1990, Amnesty International estimates that more than 5,000 political prisoners were executed.[96] According to Amnesty International, in the first eight months of 1989, of the 1,600 executions recorded worldwide, 1,200 occurred in Iran.[97] In other words, for this eight month period, Iran, with 1% of the world population, accounted for 75% of all the executions. Many of the executed during the Second Reign of Terror were political prisoners who had been arrested in the 1981-1984 period when they were in their teen or pre-teen years and had supported opposition parties. They were given jail terms, but in the months before he died, Ayatollah Khomeini had decided to cleanse prisons of political prisoners. These figures do not include those civilians who were killed by the government in indiscriminate bombings nor those who were killed in street shootouts with the coercive apparatuses of the fundamentalist regime.

The open, indiscriminate and massive repression which had character-ized fundamentalist rule from 1981 to 1989 become increasingly covert and selective between 1990 and 1997. After the election of reformist fundamen-talist, Hojatolislam Khatami in May 1997, there has been a reduction of repression.

Although all independent political parties are banned, the leadership of the secular liberal democratic Iran National Front (INF), secular nationalist Iran Nation Party (INP) and the liberal Islamist Liberation Movement of Iran (LMI) continue to meet privately despite consistent repression, harassment, numerous stints in prison and torture, as well as assassinations by agents of the Ministry of Intelligence. In June 1990, 90 members of INF, LMI and independent liberal Islamists jointly published an open letter to President Rafsanjani. In response, the fundamentalists jailed and tortured 25 of the signatories, many of whom were octogenarians who had spend years in the Shah's prisons.[98]

The actions of these respected politicians gave rise to several other open letters by public figures who criticized the restrictions on the freedoms of thought, speech and publication; many of whom were subsequently arrested, tortured, or lost their livelihood.[99] When 134 of Iran's most famous writers, poets, playwrights and intellectuals signed a politely-worded petition calling for easing of censorship of intellectual and artistic works, their publications were banned thus forcing their publishers into bankruptcy. Moreover, many of the signatories of the letter were reportedly coerced to publicly withdraw their support of the letter. In the most infamous case, Ali Akbar Saidi Sirjani, one of Iran's most respected, prolific and popular writers, died while in custody of the Intelligence Ministry, in November 1994, after publishing an open letter to Supreme Leader, Ali Khamenehi.[100]

The fundamentalist regime is also implicated in the assassination of over 60 exiled opponents of the government.[101] During an interview with the then-president Ali Akbar Hashemi Rafsanjani, Mike Wallace of the

CBS program "60 Minutes" presented Rafsanjani with a detailed list of more than 300 exiled opponents of the regime, who had been assassinated by the agents of the Iranian government.[102]

Not long after the "60 Minutes" interview, a German court convicted Iranian agents of carrying out assassinations of four leaders of the Kurdish Democratic Party of Iran who had been invited by the German Social Democratic party to attend the meeting of the Socialist International. Even more significantly, the German court, despite heavy pressure from the German Foreign Ministry that was pursuing appeasement of the fundamentalist regime, convicted Iran's top leadership for ordering these assassinations. The court ruled that the Supreme Leader (Ali Khamenehi), the President (Ali Akbar Hashemi-Rafsanjani), the Minister of Information and Intelligence (Ali Fallahian), and the Foreign Minister (Ali Akbar Velayati) had directly ordered the killings.[103]

On the night of November 22, 1998, agents of the Ministry of Intelligence entered the home of Darush and Parvaneh Forouhar, leaders of Iran Nation Party, and stabbed them to death. Darush Forouhar founded the INP and was one of the original founders of the INF along with Dr. Mossadegh in 1949. He spent 15 years in prison as political prisoner under the monarchy. After the overthrow of the Shah, Darush Forouhar became Minister of Labor in the provisional government. Parvaneh Eskandari-Forouhar, was a leading feminist and was elected to the Executive Council of the INF by the delegates to its Congress held in 1960. Parvaneh Forouhar and Dr. Homa Darabi, both liberal feminists, were the first females who had joined the leadership of a major political party in Iran. Two or three of the delegates at the 1960 INF Congress walk out in protest after Parvaneh Forouhar and Dr. Darabi sat at the table of elected leaders without hejab.[104] After the brutal murders of Darush Forouhar and Parvaneh Forouhar, about 10,000 to 15,000 mourners bravely participated in the funeral procession and shouted their support for the slain pro-democracy leaders. The mourners carried the pictures of Darush Forouhar, and Parvaneh Forouhar and Dr. Mossadegh, and shouted "Forouhar, Your Struggles Will Continue," and "Mossadegh, Forouhar, We Shall Continue Your Struggles." Under heavy popular pressure, the regime admitted that "rouge" members of the Ministry of Intelligence had committed the murders without any authorization from higher ups. The mastermind of the murders, the Deputy Minister of Intelligence, Saeed Imami was arrested; later he was pronounced dead at prison due to suicide. It is widely believed that he was killed.

By 1997, many former fundamentalists had become disillusioned with many aspects of the fundamentalist dictatorship and advocated reforms, including reduction of repression. One such person was Akbar Ganji, who became a journalist. Ganji published a series of articles implicating former President Rafsanjani (who became the powerful head of the Council of the Expediency of the System after May 1997) and Fallahian, the Minister of Intelligence in the serial murders of political opponents such as the Forouhars. Ganji was imprisoned and tortured.

Repression of High-Ranking Shia Clerics

One of the surprises of the fundamentalist rule has been the repression of the non-fundamentalist Shia clerics who constitute the majority of the clerical network. Of all the grand ayatollahs in 1979, only Khomeini supported the notion of *Velayat Faqih* (rule of the highest-ranked ulama). Grand Ayatollahs Abol-Qasem Khui, Sayyed Kazem Shariatmadari, and Haj Sayyed Hasan Tabatabai Qomi, who were the three highest ranked Shia ulama at the time, explicitly and publicly opposed Khomeini's notion of *Velayat Faqih*.[105] Khui was out of reach in Iraq, but Shariatmadari was put under house arrest where he died on 3 March 1986. His funeral was disrupted by Hezbollahi shock troops, who roughed up the mourners while Pasdaran (Islamic Revolutionary Guards) stood by.

The opposition of Grand Ayatollah Qomi was more strident and unequivocal than those of Khui and Shariatmadari. Qomi publicly opposed *Velayat Faqih*, the Constitution of the Islamic Republic, the Pasdaran, and supported Bani Sadr in his struggles against the fundamentalists. After the liberation of the border port of Khorramshahr from Iraqi military in 1982, the Iraqi forces retreated into Iraq and Saddam Hussein asked for peace. Khomeini, however, ordered the war to continue until an Islamic Republic (i.e., a pro-Iranian fundamentalist regime) was established in Iraq. Qomi issued his famous fatva declaring that henceforth anyone who either kills others or is killed in the war with Iraq will go to hell.[106] Immediately after this fatva, Qomi's son who was a hojatolislam was arrested, lashed, deturbaned and imprisoned without explanation. Since then Grand Ayatollah Qomi has been under house arrest in Mashhad.

Of more or less equal rank with Khomeini, Grand Ayatollahs Mohammad Reza Golpayegani and Shahabodin Mar'ashi Najafi were politically followers of Shariatmadari in the pre-revolutionary era. After some initial hesitation, Najafi pursued a silent course in the post-revolutionary period.[107] He did not issue any statements either in support of or in opposition to the fundamentalists. Golpayegani took a course between Najafi's quietism and Shariatmadari's restrained opposition. After a few mild criticisms of the fundamentalists, Golpayegani became unusually silent. Dr. Alireza Nurizadeh attributed this to his grandson being sentenced to death for sodomy. In exchange for allowing his grandson to quietly emigrate to England, where he now lives, Golpayegani refrained from any criticism of the ruling fundamentalists. From then until December 1993 when he died, Golpayegani remained aloof from politics.[108]

In addition, some of the most erudite ayatollahs (who were at the verge of being regarded as grand ayatollahs) such as Abdollah Shirazi, Mahmood Taleqani, Hasan Lahuti and Abolfazl Zanjani were attacked by Hezbollahi shock troops and harassed by the Pasdaran. As of this writing, the six highest-ranked living Shia ulama—Grand Ayatollahs Haj Sayyed Hasan Tabatabi Qomi, Mohammad-Hussein Sistani, Mir-Mohammad Rouhani, Sayyed Mohammad Shirazi, Hussein-Ali Montazeri, and Ya'sub al-Din Rastgari—are in opposition to the ruling fundamentalists. Sistani is out of reach in Iraq; the five who live in Iran are under house arrest.[109] Except Montazeri, all the other living Grand Ayatollahs explicitly oppose the Velayat Faqih (the rule of clerical leaders). Montazeri was the main person who formulated the concept of the rule of high ranking cleric and was one of the main authors of the fundamentalist constitution. Montazeri was chosen to replace Khomeini as the Supreme Leader, but due to his criticisms of Khomeini's order to massacre about 5,000 political prisoners in 1988, he was dismissed (about 3 months before Khomeini's death). In 2001, Montazeri publicly advocated changing the fundamentalist constitution, including eliminating the position of Supreme Leader and transferring all its powers to an elected president.[110]

Repression of Women

Perhaps the most widespread passive resistance to the fundamentalist rule has come from "apolitical" women who, in large numbers, have defied the fundamentalist regime. Women indicate their opposition to the regime by abiding by the letter of the rules on compulsory hejab but violate its spirit through wearing beautiful and colorful scarfs, leaving strands of hair out, or icing and dying their hair. According to a fundamentalist leader: "Today non-veiling and ill-veiling have become a political issue in our country.

Non-veiling and ill-veiling have become a political weapon in the hands of those who oppose the Islamic Republic."[111]

What the compulsory hejab does to keep the general public in line, the rape of female political prisoners does to control the opposition groups. According to Islamic tradition the execution of virgin girls is *makroh*.[112] Young unmarried women constitute a very large proportion of those who actively oppose the fundamentalists in power. During the First Reign of Terror in June 1981-December 1982, the government arrested a very substantial number of extremely young females. Many of these girls were in their early teens and belonged to the communist Islamist PMOI and to the communist groups Fadaian and Paykar.[113] The government went ahead with the execution of these girls.[114] According to numerous reports, when returning the corpses of the executed girls to their families, a small sum of money was included as "mehryeh." According to several sources, the government waited until the girls reached their ninth birthday; then they were allowed to be raped and then executed.[115] In the words of Suroosh Irfani:

Islamic judges believed that carrying out the death sentence against virgin females was 'un-Islamic'. It is believed that the troubled conscience of such Islamic judges was pacified when one Islamic authority ruled that the virgin girls sentenced to death could be married off to Islamic Revolutionary Guards for a few hours. After defloration by their temporary husbands, the girls could then be executed 'Islamically' without pangs of religious conscientiousness. However, according to another religious decree issued by Khomeini, those women and girls who are arrested and imprisoned against charges of 'waging war against God', are automatically regarded as 'spoils of war'. This decree makes it religiously acceptable for the Islamic Revolutionary Guards and torturers of the girls to rape them.[116]

In a well-known case the fundamentalists executed 11 girls who were under 16 years of age. These girls, who were supporters of the PMOI, refused to give their names and simply identified themselves as "Mojahed" (singular form of the word Mojahedin in Farsi) and daughter of "the Iranian people." After they were executed, the fundamentalists published their photos in a newspaper and asked their parents to come and claim them.[117]

When confronted with justifying the execution of young teenage girls Ayatollah Mohammad Gilani, who was Tehran's Revolutionary Prosecutor at the time said that, "...on the basis of Islam a nine-year-old girl is considered mature. So there is no difference for us between a nine-year-old girl and a 40-year-old man, and it does not prohibit us from issuing any kind of sentence."[118] In the words of Ayatollah Hussein Moussavi-Tabrizi, the revolutionary prosecutor-general, "We cannot practice forgiveness or leniency... when faced with so many people."[119]

Also related to this issue is the reported rape of young daughters of political prisoners as well as the torture of young sons in order to force confessions (and perhaps information). Helmut Szimkus, the German engineer who spent five years (1989-94) in Evin Prison on charges of spying for Iraq (which he later admitted to when freed) was witness to many such incidents of torture. In an interview he granted to the German magazine, *Focus*, Szimkus reported: "One time these guys (the torturers) raped a nine-year-old girl.... The parents had to watch... the father shook and rattled so badly that he could no longer sign the espionage confession they put before him."[120] Szimkus added, "Once they took on a boy. Do you know how an innocent child screams when he is tortured? His parents were right there in the next cell, it drove them up the wall."[121]

A report published by the Human Rights Group of the British Parliament (House of Commons) quotes from Mr. Sarmast Akhlagh Tabandeh, a former prosecutor of the Revolutionary Guards in Shiraz, as saying:

> The general rule is that virgin girls have to be sexually raped prior to execution. The prison administrators write the names of the Revolutionary Guard members of the firing squad as well as the names of administrators present on pieces of paper and a lottery is held among these names. ...The night before execution, a sedative drug is injected into the virgin girl and the winning Guard would rape her. ...The day after the execution the prison Shariah judge sends a marriage certificate along with a box of pastries to the family of the girl.[122]

It appears that the fundamentalist ulama engage in the enforcement of the compulsory veil, repression of dissent, torture of political prisoners and the rape of female political prisoners, not as dictates of Islamic dogma but because doing so strengthens them and helps them remain in power. According to Ali Banuazizi:

> ...the government's relentless 'Islamization' campaign has extended its control (often through the use of gangs of thugs and 'Party of God' troopers) into all spheres of public and private life. This has led to some of the greatest abuses of human rights, particularly toward women and

members of religious minorities. While for the more dogmatically fundamentalist members of the regime the main objective remains the implementation of an absolutist vision of Islam through a 'cultural revolution', for others, and perhaps the majority within the regime, the objective is simply to hold on to power at whatever cost.[123]

CONCLUSION

A man may—and indeed many do—use the **threat** of polygyny, contracting sigheh, and divorce to subordinate his wife. Considering the socio-economic and political milieu of post-revolution Iran (i.e., the lack of jobs for women, absence of social security benefits, dismissal of employed urban women, limits on women's access to higher education) in addition to the re-established Shariah law which grants sole custody of children to the father (who can and usually does deny any visitation by the mother) a woman has few options but to submit to a man's every whim.

Many women, including illiterate women, realize the patriarchal ramifications of post-revolution legal changes. Anthropologist Erika Friedl who conducted field work among rural villagers concluded that these rural women:

> ...express real anguish and dread. Women fail to see any moral good connected with these laws, no redeeming religious or spiritual value whatsoever, either in this or in the next world. Rather, they take the laws very practically as an effective undermining of their position vis-a-vis their husbands and a strengthening of the man's position at the woman's expense. No matter what the mullahs say, religion is thus seen as being used to support men and to oppress women.[124]

The implementation of fundamentalist policies in conjunction with the socio-economic and political conditions of Iran created the golden cage of which Frye spoke. Early post-revolutionary laws and policies such as those on polygyny, sigheh, divorce, child custody, hejab rules, the firing of women, restrictions on higher education and employment for women, and lack of social security benefits, are the golden bars of the cage in the analogy.

From February 1979 and 1984, Ayatollah Khomeini and the fundamentalist elites succeeded in establishing extremely misogynist laws based on the letter of Shariah. Everything that Khomeini and the fundamentalists did had their sources in the letter of the Quran, Hadith and the actual deeds of Shia Imams. For fundamentalists this was a major achievement, whereas for others it was a grave injustice, one for which Islam was blamed. The analytically significant question is: What is the relationship between Islam and Khomeini's misogynist policies? Are these misogynist policies the inevitable product of Islam?

Figure 2-1: The number of men per 100 women in Iran

	Male	Female	No. of Men per 100 Women
1956 (1335)	9,644,944	9,309,760	104
1966 (1345)	13,355,801	12,432,921	107
1976 (1355)	17,356,347	16,352,397	106
1986 (1365)	25,280,961	24,164,049	105

Source: Census data provided in Islamic Republic of Iran, Plan and Budget Organization, Statistical Centre of Iran, , Table 2-1, p. 33.

Figure 2-2: Unemployment rates for men and women in urban areas before and after the revolution; all numbers (except those in last column) are in thousands

	Economically Active Population			
	Total	Employed	Unemployed Seeking Job	Unemployment Rate
Women 1976	489	460	29	5.9
Men 1976	3,846	3,653	194	5.0
Women 1986	741	525	216	29.1
Men 1986	6,285	5,428	857	13.6

Source: The results in the right column are my calculations based on 1976 and 1986 census data provided in Islamic Republic of Iran, Plan and Budget Organization, Statistical Centre of Iran, *Iran Statistical Yearbook 1369 [March 1990-March 1991]*, (in Farsi), Table 3-1, p. 62. All the data are for 10-year-olds and older. Unemployment rate is defined as those who are unemployed and are actively seeking employment as percentage of all the economically active population. Students, homemakers and others classified as non-economically active are included in the census data as separate categories under non-economically active population (which enhances the integrity of these calculations).

Figure 2-3: Employed as percentage of total population 10-years-old and older in urban areas before and after the revolution; all numbers (except those in last column) are in thousands

	Employed	Total Population 10-years-old & Older	Employed as % of Population 10 Years-old & Older
Women 1976	460	5,410	8.5
Men 1976	3,653	6,018	60.7
Women 1986	525	8,869	5.9
MEN 1986	5,428	9,412	57.7

Source: The results in the right column are my calculations based on 1976 and 1986 census data provided in Islamic Republic of Iran, Plan and Budget Organization, Statistical Centre of Iran, *Iran Statistical Yearbook 1369 [March 1990-March 1991]*, (in Farsi), Table 3-1, p. 62.

CHAPTER 3

THEORIES OF GENDER AND
POLITICAL PARTIES 1979–1984

The purpose of this chapter is to demonstrate that Islam is neither the necessary condition nor the sufficient condition for the fundamentalists' gender inegalitarian policies described in the previous chapter. In the section on anti-feminism, I demonstrate that anti-feminism is shared by many groups, ideologies and religions; therefore, Islam is not the necessary condition for gender inequality. In the sections on liberal feminism, traditional Marxism, radical feminism, and socialist feminism I demonstrate that there were (and are) Iranian political groups (both Islamist and secular) with feminist ideologies which have struggled to implement feminist demands; therefore, demonstrating that Islam (as ideology, religion, and civilization) is not a sufficient condition for gender inequality.

It is not my intention to present a comprehensive exposition of feminist theories because many such works already exist.[1] Instead, relying upon the existing literature I will summarize views of "anti-feminism," "liberal feminism," "traditional Marxism," "radical feminism," and "socialist feminism." In Figures 3-1 and 3-2, I have sketched a simplified, unidimensional historiography of political ideas.

ANTI-FEMINISM

Anti-feminists believe that men and women are essentially so different, especially biologically and psychologically, that their roles in society cannot but be correspondingly different. Men are more rational, more aggressive, more ruthless; therefore, political and economic realms which demand cut-throat competition are preserved as men's domain. On the other hand, women are emotional, nurturing, empathetic, and less rational; therefore, women are more suited to a family realm. A good society should pass laws which protect women from the drudgery of work outside the home and compel men to take care of "their" women. Women and men should have **different** political, economic and social roles, rights and privileges. Women in the Western tradition were denied the right to own and manage property on these grounds.[2]

Today, many contemporary conservatives are only partially anti-feminist. Most *bona fide* anti-feminists tend to be either religious fundamentalists or fascists. According to Haleh Afshar, Khomeini's views on women are similar to those of Hitler and Mussolini; she further cites identical policies pursued by these regimes.[3] Farah Azari, an Iranian socialist feminist scholar, argues that the class, gender and psychological roots of German Nazis and Iranian Islamic fundamentalists are similar.[4] According to Adolf Hitler, "The wonderful thing about nature and providence is that no conflict between the sexes can occur as long as each party performs the function prescribed for it by nature."[5] Valentine Moghadam argues that this quote from Hitler "could equally have been uttered by a right-wing anti-abortion activist in the United States, an Islamic fundamentalist in Iran or Algeria, an orthodox Jew in Israel...."[6]

According to Hojatolislam Ali-Akbar Hashemi Rafsanjani, who has been and continues to be one of the top three most powerful members of the fundamentalist ruling elite in Iran, "Pregnancy and taking care of children by women are the two essential duties of women.... These two duties have been assigned to women based on the *khelghat* [divine creation] and the laws of nature."[7] According to Eliz Sanasarian, "the Moral Majority" is "a group that has views concerning women somewhat similar to those of the Islamic Republic."[8] I will demonstrate in the following sections of this chapter that there are substantial differences between Islamic fundamentalists on the one hand and non-fundamentalist Islamists on the other.[9]

It is important to mention here that both men **and** women can be anti-feminists. Many women, such as Dr. Phyllis Schlafly, Mrs. Farideh Zahra

Mostafavi (Khomeini's daughter and the Secretary-General of the state-sanctioned "Society of Women of the Islamic Republic"), argue that women in their protected traditional position would be better off than in the equal but insecure position proposed by feminists. These women believe that feminists are misguided and that feminism leads to disillusionment, misery and loneliness.[10] Anti-feminists strongly support both governmental programs that would protect the traditional family (i.e., patriarchal family) and family wage for **men** so that they can take care of "their" women and children.[11]

According to Phyllis Schlafly, the most "cruel and damaging sexual harassment taking place today" is "by feminists and their federal government allies against the role of motherhood and the role of the dependent wife."[12] According to Rev. Jerry Falwell, one of the leaders of American anti-feminist Christian fundamentalism, children have the right:

> ...to have the love of a mother and a father who understand their different roles and fulfill their different responsibilities.... To live in an economic system that makes it possible for husbands to support their wives as full time mothers in the home and that enables families to survive on one income instead of two.[13]

According to Afsaneh Najmabadi, anti-feminists in Iran argue that:

> ...what is upheld as equality of rights in Western societies is in fact similarity of rights, and that women's quest for such similarity is both immoral and unjust, running contrary to the divine plan as well as the natural disposition of women. In their view, women and men are created differently and are suitable for different roles in their social and private lives.[14]

The single most influential Islamic fundamentalist leader on women's issues was Ayatollah Morteza Mottahari, who was the Chairman of the Revolutionary Council which ruled Iran immediately after the overthrow of the Shah. In his book *Women's Rights in Islam*, which has become the canon in the Islamic Republic, Mottahari states:

> It is certain that man and woman in Islam do not have identical rights. The West attempts to create an identical situation for man and woman with regard to laws, rights, and duties, thus ignoring the natural differences between the sexes. Here lies the distinction between Islam and Western

systems of thought. Until the twentieth century European women had not been awarded either legal or human rights. As a result of an inadequately reasoned movement that arose in the name of women's liberation, rights were given to women more or less identical to those of men. But women, because of their natural condition and their physical and mental disposition, cannot reach equality with men. Man and woman can only attain happiness when they are accorded rights appropriate and peculiar to themselves. If we wish to liberate ourselves from the blind imitation of Western philosophy, we must first establish whether equality of rights implies identity of rights, for equality is not identity. It is quite natural that man protects woman and woman seeks protection from man. It is not necessary to look for a social or historical reason on which to base this. Why is man physically stronger and woman weaker and more delicate? This physical difference does not exist only between man and woman, but between cock and hen, lion and lioness, stallion and mare. This was the intention of God, an intention that was totally left out of account by Western feminists who believe that both sexes should receive the same training and assume the same professions and social responsibilities. But the truth is that woman is distinct from man in various ways. Every cell of her body, her entire organism and especially her nervous system, is characterized by her female gender. Physiological laws like astronomic laws are fixed, immutable principles. The human will has no influence upon them whatsoever. We must accept them as they are. Therefore women should attempt to develop the innate capabilities that correspond to their own nature.[15]

For Islamic fundamentalists, the argument that there are natural (and psychological) differences between men and women is justification that there should be differences in political rights, duties and responsibilities between men and women.[16] The Constitution, written by the fundamentalists in 1979, put into law that women cannot hold the positions of president and prime minister. During the constitutional proceedings, some non-fundamentalists had apparently opposed *de jure* exclusion of women from these positions. In response, Ayatollah Sadughi (Khomeini's powerful representative in central Iran and a member of the convention known as Assembly of Experts) argued: "Now suppose we appointed one of these fully competent women as president or prime minister. Then one morning we will wake up to find the prime ministry closed. Why? Because last night she was giving birth. This would be scandalous for us. For God's sake do not allow this to become law."[17]

In the 1960s, Ayatollah Khomeini had explicitly and publicly opposed the enfranchisement of women and their right to hold office.[18] When in 1962 the Shah wanted to enfranchise women, Ayatollah Khomeini sent a cable to Prime Minister Alam stating that, "The ulama made it public that women's franchise and the abrogation of the condition to be a Muslim to be allowed to elect or to be elected is contrary to Islam and the constitution."[19] According to Ayatollah Khomeini, women's suffrage was "unacceptable from a religious point of view" and a step towards "the spread of corruption and prostitution among women."[20]

Khomeini also regarded membership in the Majles (in the 1960s) to be a male prerogative. In Khomeini's words, "Can you attain progress by sending a few women to the parliament? ...We say that sending women to these places will lead to nothing but corruption.... We are not against women's progress, we oppose this prostitution, and these wrong measures."[21] In addition, in his famous October 27, 1964, statement (which caused his arrest and deportation) Khomeini said that "the ruling clique is bent... upon insisting on employing women in government offices to spread corruption."[22]

However, after coming to power, Ayatollah Khomeini was very careful not to use language which **explicitly** assigned inferior positions and status to women. Instead, he borrowed the language of "difference" from Ayatollah Mottahari. For example, the Ministry of National Guidance quotes Ayatollah Khomeini as saying, "Women are not equal to men, but neither are men equal to women.... Their roles in society are complementary.... Each has certain distinct functions according to his or her nature and constitution."[23]

Zan-e Rouz, the semi-official women's weekly which reflects the regime's latest policy on the "women's question," stated in an editorial:

Colonialism was fully aware of the sensitive and vital role of women in the formation of the individual and of human society. They considered her the best tool for subjugation of the nations. Therefore, under such pretexts as social activity, the arts, freedom, etc., they pushed her to degeneracy and degradation and made of her a doll who not only forgot her human role, but became the best tool for emptying others of their humanity.... In Western societies where capitalism is dominant... women's liberation is nothing but the liberty to be naked, to prostitute oneself.... In the underdeveloped countries... women serve as the unconscious accomplices of the powers-that-be in the destruction of indigenous culture. So long as indigenous culture persists in the personality and thought of people in a society, it is not easy to find a political, military, economic or social presence in that society.... And woman is the best means of destroying the indigenous culture to the benefit of imperialists.[24]

The image of women projected by this editorial is that of Eve at the garden of Eden.[25] The modern Satan is the imperialist West that can only corrupt this pure society through the woman. Women's liberation and equality is considered as dangerous and as an indication of treason and collusion with Satan. The indigenous culture which assigns an inferior position to women is the only weapon that can protect the political, military, economic and social interests of the society. As the following quote illustrates, the only solution is forcing women to wear the veil—and, symbolically, accepting Islamic patriarchal controls on women:

> In Islamic countries the role of women is even more sensitive. Islamic belief and culture provides people of these societies with faith and ideals.... Woman in these societies is armed with a shield that protects her against the conspiracies aimed at her humanity, honor and chastity. This shield is verily her veil. For this reason... the most immediate and urgent task was seen to be unveiling.... Then she became the target of poisonous arrows of corruption, prostitution, nakedness, looseness, and trivialities. After this, she was used to disfigure the Islamic culture of the society, to erase people's faith and drag society in her wake toward corruption, decay and degradation.
>
> ...It is here that we realize the glory and depth of Iran's Islamic Revolution.... Today the Muslim woman has well understood... that the only way for her social presence to be healthy and constructive is to use Islamic veil and cloths....[26]

Ideas and ideologies become mobilizing when they express in ideal forms the interests of certain strata. Patriarchal ideologies, while at one level specific to geographical place and time, also have universal aspects with reference to class and gender interests. It should come as no surprise that males in insecure jobs would be attracted to fascistic and religious fundamentalist ideologies which promise a male dominated society; the return of women to the home entails more job security in the job market and a restored male authority at home. The following quote is illustrative. The interviewee is Dennis McGiffen who is the highest-ranking Ku Klux Klan organizer in the state of Illinois.

McGiffen: ...We don't want to destroy the government. We don't want to do away with the government. We want to be the government.

Reporter: And what would the country be like if the KKK were the government?

McGiffen: Oh, it would be a haven for white people. It would be a haven. I believe we would all be working, and we'd have jobs to support our families where our wives wouldn't have to go out and work. Our wives could take care of the children and we could stop having illegitimate children running the streets.
    ...We have a lot of confrontation, especially with the homosexuals. They know how we feel about them. It's in the Bible. We go by Bible laws. And the homosexuals know that's it's the death penalty to the homosexuals. That's just the way we feel.[27]

Some Islamic fundamentalists explicitly argue that men are superior to women and base their arguments on specific Koranic verses. Hojatolislam Abbas Abbasi, who is a member of the Fourth Majles from Bandar Abbas, after citing verses from the Koran concluded that, "Women have to accept that men are their rulers [masters] and the world has to know that men are superior."[28]
    Not all anti-feminists argue that males are superior to females. Assuming that women are not equipped to compete successfully against men in society, anti-feminists believe that women would be better off being taken care of at home. In other words, an inferior position within patriarchy is preferable to an insecure one within a competitive dynamic society. It was these beliefs, some argue, that led the Iranian fundamentalists to pass laws forbidding full-time work for all mothers of young children and curtailing day-care centers.[29] Likewise, American Christian fundamentalists have strongly condemned day-care and the ERA.[30]
    What should be clear from the discussion in this section is that many of the belief systems of the Islamic fundamentalists with regards to gender are not exclusively Islamic and that they are shared by other anti-feminists in other cultures and religions. In other words, what has been considered to be Islamic in nature, or even Islamic fundamentalist in essence, is shared by other religions. To be more precise, Islam is not a necessary condition for anti-feminism.
    For instance, the ideology of domesticity prevalent among Islamic fundamentalists is remarkably similar, if not identical, to those held by

Christian fundamentalists. If the privileging of the roles of wife and mother is a shared element among Nazis, fascists, Christian fundamentalists and Islamic fundamentalists, then Islam is not the independent variable explaining the existence of the notion of domesticity. In other words, because the notion of domesticity (the importance of the role of mother-hood and wife) exists in many ideologies and groups, its existence cannot be explained by reference to Islam. If Islam was the independent variable causing the existence of the belief in domesticity, then non-Islamic ideologies would not contain this belief.

It is also important to note that the belief in domesticity is not exclusive to the above-mentioned groups; to various degrees it is shared by many other groups and perhaps, in a diffuse form, by the populace in large. In 1873, for example, the U.S. Supreme Court, in a case which upheld the denial of the right of women to practice law said:

> The civil law, as well as nature herself, has always recognized a wide difference in the respective spheres and destinies of man and woman. Man is, or should be, woman's protector and defender. The natural and proper timidity and delicacy which belongs to the female sex evidently unfits it for many of the occupations of civil life. The constitution of the family organization, which is founded in the divine ordinance, as well as in the nature of things, indicates the domestic sphere as that which properly belongs to the domain and functions of womanhood. The harmony, not to say identity, of interests and views which belong, or should belong, to the family institution is repugnant to the idea of a woman adopting a distinct and independent career from that of her husband.... The paramount destiny and mission of women are to fulfill the noble and benign offices of wife and mother. This is the law of the Creator.[31]

There are also a plethora of gender issues which are usually considered to be the dependent variable, being caused by Islam. Prime among these are sex-segregation and the inferior position of women in the mosque. The fact is that many orthodox Jewish groups also have segregated seating arrangements not only in their synagogues but also at communal ceremonies, such as weddings. Moreover, orthodox and fundamentalist Jewish women have to shave their heads and/or have them covered in public. In addition, prior to Vatican II, women in the Catholic church had to cover their heads and their voices could not be heard while in mass. In the previous chapter, I argued that because we witness *de facto* polygyny both in Islamic and Latin American countries (which are Catholic), Islam can not be regarded as the necessary condition for polygyny. Rather, patriarchal groups may utilize Islam to legitimize men's privileged sexual access to women and deny women similar privilege. In other words, men, particularly wealthy men can have access to several women but wealthy women do not have that right both in Islamic and Catholic Latin American polities. The fact of *de facto* polygyny is the same, but the specific contours of polygyny are shaped by Islam in one context and by cultural norms in the other.

From the discussion in this section we can conclude that: many beliefs and notions that are considered Islamic are shared by other religious and secular groups. Hence, insofar as anti-feminist practices and ideas are shared by various groups, one could conclude that Islam is not the causal factor (necessary condition) but rather it is the medium through which anti-feminism is expressed.

LIBERAL FEMINISM

Liberal feminism can be considered to be an intellectual descendant of classical liberalism; its roots are easily traced to that tradition. Mary Wollstonecraft, Abigail Adams, John Stuart Mill and Harriet Taylor Mill included women in Lockean liberalism's notion of the rights of man.[32] Succinctly put, contemporary liberal feminists believe in capitalism in economics and liberal democracy in the political arena. They differ from other liberals in the sense that they would like to see women represented in equal proportions in all facets of the public realm. Their ideal society, for example, is one in which half of the businesspeople, lawyers, members of legislatures and chief executives are women. Liberal feminists simply ask for equality of opportunity for women. It is hoped that in the long run, with the presumed equality of men and women a gender-equal society would emerge.

According to liberal feminists, a person's sex should not be considered a factor in political and economic discrimination or in inhibiting one's potential.[33] In other words, liberal feminists do not oppose hierarchy in society; they merely argue that one's sex is not a legitimate reason for an inferior position in a non-egalitarian system. Liberal feminists, like other contemporary liberals, advocate juridical equality for all, and equality of opportunity for all. They do not advocate equality of end-result.

In legal terminology, discrimination based on sex is a "suspect" category. A resolution of the National Organization for Women, the major liberal feminist group in the U.S., declared as its goal, "...to bring women into full participation in the mainstream of American society *now*, exercising all the privileges and responsibilities thereof in truly equal partnership with men."[34]

In order to achieve their goals, liberal feminists advocate: (1) legal reforms; (2) a change in gender role socialization; and (3) certain positive governmental policies aiding women. In the first category, one may include the demand for female suffrage, civil rights and equal opportunity legislation. The second category includes avoiding or ceasing the inculcation of different values in boys and girls. Boys are taught to be competitive, assertive and to withhold emotional expressions (with the exception of anger); girls are taught contrasting values of nurturance, supportiveness, and that it is acceptable to show emotion. Boys are told that "men do not cry"; little girls are allowed to do so. Little boys are encouraged to be tough and adventurous; girls are given frilly pink dresses that limit the possibilities for becoming dirty. At college or at work, aggressive, selfish, unyielding men are regarded as "competitive and assertive" whereas women with the same characteristics are regarded negatively. Society and social norms encourage and perpetuate these different mores between the sexes. Liberal feminists believe that it is possible to modify these norms and to provide one set of norms for both sexes.[35]

Parenthetically, I should add that I believe there is a schism among liberal feminists on this issue. Some, like Virginia Woolf, Carol Gilligan, and Judith Stiehm seem to believe that men's nature and women's nature are different, and women should **not** want to become just like men.[36] Female values of compassion, nurturance, cooperation, and empathy are superior to male values of aggressiveness, selfishness, arrogance, violence and domination. Other groups of liberal feminists believe that men's and women's psychological make-up (and their nature) are similar, or that socialization is **the** differentiating factor, or the effect of socialization is far greater than merely any biological differences.[37] Regardless of their views on the relative importance of socialization, all liberal feminists oppose any law which restricts women's equal rights to compete against men in whatever endeavor is chosen.

Lastly, liberal feminists advocate certain positive public policies such as state-funded (or, in the case of large corporations, company-funded) child-care centers and maternity leave. Some liberal feminists also advocate affirmative action and **paid** maternity leave (which might be considered a departure from a strict definition of equality of opportunity). These measures are needed not because women are inferior and need protection but because family structure and tradition force women to care for children, thereby hampering their ability to succeed in the marketplace. Furthermore, feminists argue that since all societies need to reproduce themselves, women are performing a service for society by having babies and hence should be rewarded, not penalized, for performing a socially necessary function.

Islamic fundamentalism explicitly opposes liberal feminist assumptions and programs; one of the first post-revolutionary policies was the closing of many day-care centers. This move was based on the argument that they are "an imperialist plot" which would promote women's separation from their essential role in society as mothers by allowing them to work.[38]

Liberal feminist groups by definition oppose Islamic fundamentalism; among the more prominent of these are "Women's Organization of the National Front (WONF)," "Women Adherents of Freedom Movement of Iran," and "The Union of Women Lawyers."[39] Because the Women's Organization of the National Front is the oldest, largest and the most influential liberal feminist group in Iran, I quote its views extensively. In an open letter and a call to a protest rally against the dismissal of female judges it declared:

> ...no efforts must be spared so that women can participate in all aspects of the society with the preservation of their eminent human character. Society must provide all the necessary conditions for the flourishing of women's talents as well as their mobilization in the construction of the country, so that they can live and work shoulder to shoulder with men in equality.
>
> ...Throughout the Revolution, one principle has been demanded by all social classes and sections more than any other, and that is 'freedom' and 'equality'. Now, in the dawn of victory, freedom and equality, irrespective of class and sex is being threatened.
>
> ...The content of the Declaration of Human Rights has been again and again supported by all freedom-lovers of this country. Now it seems that the intentions of the Declaration are being violated and are losing their credibility. One instance of the Declaration is the freedom of choice of occupation. The meaning of this is that everybody has the right to choose his or her occupation, irrespective of sex. We consider this the right of a woman to reach to the position she deserves. One of the important instances of the violation of human rights by the present government is the question of practice of law by women. WONF supports the rights of women to practice law and considers the indifference shown by the

government as an insult to all heroic and militant women of Iran. WONF, in support of women's rights, will participate in the protest gathering in Tehran University on 2 May 1979, and invites all supporters of just demands of women lawyers also to do so.[40]

In April 1979, Khomeini issued a decree ordering the dismissal of all female judges, arguing that it was against Islam. The INF (Iran's main secular liberal democratic party) was the only organization that defended the right of women to be judges. Neither the communists, nor the PMOI, nor any other organization wanted to stand up to Khomeini at that particular juncture.

The following is an excerpt from an article published on March 1, 1981, in the organ of the INF, parent organization of the WONF. It states:

> Not only does women's share in the Constitution suffer from deficiencies and inadequacies... the election procedures of the Assembly of Experts and the Consultative Assembly were such that women could not have much of a role in them. Women are not taken into account in job responsibilities and social tasks; legislation such as the special civil [family] courts have weakened her situation within the family; compulsion and force have been used to determine what she should look like in public; the purges of the ministries have mostly affected women; in the Bill of Retribution (aside from principle criticisms regarding this law) her share has been weakness, inferiority and inequality; ...[in addition to all this] in the society as a whole women are not treated as human beings, she has been deprived of all the gifts, the blessings, and the favors bestowed upon her by Islam that she expected as a matter of course in the aftermath of the people's Revolution....[41]

It is significant to add that although most supporters of WONF were secular, they were not atheists. In other words, many of their members considered themselves to be simultaneously good Muslims and liberal feminists. The members of the "Women Adherents of the Freedom Movement," on the other hand, were explicitly Islamist and liberal feminist; they did not believe that there was any inherent contradiction between Islamic government and women's rights.[42] Therefore, because practicing Muslims in the INF and LMI are also consciously liberal feminists we can conclude that Islam is not a sufficient condition for anti-feminism. It is perceptions of reality that determine behavior, and not the actual reality. Whether the text of the Quran is anti-feminist or not is less of analytical significance here than what is the perception of those who regard them-selves as Muslims. The analytically significant point is that many members of the INF and LMI believed that their Islam was compatible with their feminism.

TRADITIONAL MARXISM/MARXIST FEMINISM

The labels "traditional Marxism" and "Marxist feminism" are used interchangeably in this book. Tong follows this terminology, whereas others such as Jagger and Rothenberg classify "Marxist feminism" and "socialist feminism" together in contradistinction to "traditional Marxism." This typology is **not** accidental. Like Tong, I consider Marx and Engels to have given consideration to gender as a variable.[43] Marxism gives primary importance to class and class struggle since the development of private property; it subsumes gender as a concept in class; and, it regards "feminist struggle" as secondary (and, at worst, as divisive) to class struggle. For Marxists, a bourgeois woman has a lot more in common with a bourgeois man than with a proletarian woman. There does **not** exist such a thing as patriarchy. Capital and capitalists divide the working class along many lines: gender, race, ethnicity, nation, country, religion, white-collar/blue-collar, etc. Once capitalism is superseded, Marxists argue, all these secondary problems—sexism, racism, nationalism, bigotry—will lose their material base and disappear. Sexism is simply one weapon, among many, that capitalists use to "divide and conquer" the working class. According to Marxists, women are superexploited because they not only are exploited as wage labor but also because they are underpaid. The cause of the under-payment is located in the superstructural reasons such as family responsi-bility. These superstructural reasons are caused by the structural base "which was unquestionably to be found in the extraction of surplus value by capital from wage labor at the point of production."[44]

Traditional Marxists (or Marxist feminists) consider Engels' *Origin of the Family* to explain the inferior position of women from the dawn of civilization up to the present age in every society.[45] Some feminists (especially radical feminists such as Firestone) have criticized it as economic reductionism and as uni-dimensional, a book which analyzes a woman's situation only within the economic sphere and which totally neglects the biological causes of subordination.[46]

The interpretation presented here differs from the two positions mentioned above. I argue that: (1) Engels provides a **conceptual framework** that includes both relations of material production and relations of human reproduction; and (2) Engels unduly subordinates the private realm and reproduction to the public realm and production in his **analysis** of the subordination of women.

In the preface to the first edition of his book, Engels writes:

> According to the materialistic conception, the determining factor in history is, in the final instance, the production and **reproduction** of immediate life. This, again, is of a twofold character: on the one side, the production of the means of existence, of food, clothing and shelter and the tools necessary for that production; on the other side, the **production of human beings themselves, the propagation of the species.** The social organization under which the people of a particular historical epoch and a particular country live is determined by both kinds of production: by the stage of development of Labour on the one hand and of **the family on the other.**[47]

In these words, Engels has made it clear that **two factors** determine (most of the time) the social organization of life: (1) the economic organization of production; and (2) the social organization of both the family structure and the social construction of the female childbearing function.

From the above passage, it is clear that the radical feminists' charge, that Engels does not provide **categories** for analyzing patriarchy, is false. However, their charge that he does not deal with patriarchy is partially true. Engels considers the nuclear family to be oppressive, that housework is analogous to slavery, that men (in the family but not outside) oppress women, and that in order for women to be emancipated, economic equality is not enough.[48] He fails to understand, though, that the sexual division of labor does not occur only in the family but also exists in the sphere of production.[49] There is a great deal of sex-segregation in the labor market: in other words, even when men and women participate in the paid labor force, they do not engage in the same jobs in the same proportions.[50]

By recognizing oppression of women **only** in the family, Engels misses the reality of societal dichotomy of power, that men as a whole oppress women as a whole. Engels' oversight becomes critical when the ramifications of his theory are analyzed. Engels' solution is to bring women into the paid labor force and to abolish the nuclear family. If patriarchal relations and ideology were still prevalent, it would be women who would get most of the low-paying jobs, including the paid housework, and it would be men who would still control the most important positions of authority and power.[51]

In Engels' analysis, women's biology plays an important role only **before** the appearance of private property. Indeed, he argues, "The first division of labour is that between man and woman for the propagation of children."[52] After private property enters the scene, women's situations are essentially analyzed on the basis of women's relation to the means of production, not their reproductive role in society. Engels analyzes the bourgeois family as though both sexes share the same consciousness, security, life opportunities, etc. This is the main deficiency of Engels' analysis; a bourgeois woman's power is vicarious, not direct.[53] He misses the fact that these "bourgeois" women cannot realize their potential as "species-being" because the patriarchal ideology and structure prevent them from realizing their humanity. Women simply as women, regardless of their husbands' class, share certain similarities such as their role in the propagation of human beings, their stabilizing role in the family, etc.

Engels provides the conceptual framework for analyzing society based on both relations of production and reproduction, but he fails to give due account to the relation of reproduction when he analyzes capitalist society.

It is important to point out here that all Iranian Marxist-Leninist parties and organizations shared the traditional Marxist feminist view of the "women's question."[54] Following the Comintern in theory and practice, Iranian Marxist-Leninist parties established various front organizations; sometimes the links to the parent party were publicly stated and sometimes they were covert. Almost all Marxist-Leninist parties in Iran established their own women's groups. Unlike the "ideal" notion of "transition belt," which is supposed to be a two-way communication—transmitting the directives of the parent party to the various "democratic organizations" **and** also to lobby and inform the party of the particular interests of the group (e.g., women's interests)—the primary, if not the sole, task of the women's groups became the recruitment of new members for the parent organization and the propagation of the ideological niche of the parent party.[55] Peykar, the second largest Marxist-Leninist party in Iran, argued:

> The democratic organization which we have in mind is one that does not becloud class contradictions, but will rather make the uncompromising

army of the proletariate ever more united by organizing toiling women around the democratic goals of the proletariate. According to this principle, any organization which seeks to organize toiling women around slogans such as "women's general issues" and "women's common grievances" and to obfuscate existing contradictions among antagonistic classes, and consequently cause a class compromise, or to advocate that securing women's denied-rights, which requires proletarian leadership and can be achieved only in a socialist society, can indeed be accomplished in a capitalist society is a deviationist organization and shall have no function but to misguide and waste women's fighting spirit and shall betray and serve the bourgeoisie.[56]

As has been argued by others, such analyses led to a plethora of positions among the parties of the left ranging from indifference and ambivalence by some to outright antagonism by others towards the independent women's movement.[57] The traditional left's ideological orientation (in addition to the opportunism of some) may explain why the leadership of leftist parties did not help women resist the compulsory veil in March 1979, or the dismissal of female judges in March 1979. The leftist parties were quick to agree with the fundamentalist propaganda that these women were bourgeois, liberal or Monarchist. The Tudeh party, for example, went so far as to call Khomeini the most dedicated supporter of women's rights and warned that, "The sensitive questions of women is one of the areas where counterrevolutionary and bigoted elements have pinned their hopes for weakening the revolution."[58] This statement was made after Khomeini came to power and launched the most misogynist policies in Iranian history. The Tudeh party, however, reversed these glowing remarks after 1983 when the fundamentalist elite decided to arrest, torture and/or execute the Tudeh leadership.

During the perilous early post-revolutionary times in the 1979-1982 period, the Fadaian considered the women's question to be a "secondary" issue which—along with its consideration of civil liberties as bourgeois rights—led to ambivalence and hesitation towards Khomeini's policies. For Fadaian, class and imperialism were the most important contradictions in society; therefore, Khomeini's onslaughts against women's rights and civil liberties were overlooked because Khomeini was perceived to be anti-capitalist and anti-imperialist. At the theoretical level, Fadaian considered gender to be subsumed under class. The Fadaian covertly sponsored a women's group which claimed to be independent but acted as a transmission belt for its politburo. According to their women's front:

We do not consider our emancipation separate from the emancipation of the toiling classes, and therefore considered the establishment of a direct link with deprived classes, investigation of their working conditions and the health and welfare of working women, as our primary task and responsibility. Also, the promotion of cultural and political consciousness of the working classes was one of our essential programmes.[59]

Although the Fadaian acknowledged the existence of discrimination against women, they considered the source of this oppression to be superstructural and that there was no need for an independent women's movement because "freedom is a humanitarian goal which is not determined by sex."[60] In retrospect, this group admitted that the "Lack of attention paid by the communist movement as a whole to the question of woman's position and her oppression in the society" as well as the apathy of working-class women themselves toward women's rights were responsible for the failure of the resistance to the Islamic fundamentalist regime's misogynistic policies.[61]

The most interesting case of an Iranian political party associated with Marxist feminist views, and certainly the one most analytically salient for our discussion, is that of the "Islamic communist" group, the PMOI.[62] The PMOI was established in 1965 as an underground guerrilla organization. Its ideology is called "Jame'e Be-Tabagheh Towhidi," which means "Classless Divine Society." By classless society, the PMOI referred to the societies that had been established in USSR and communist China. In 1972, in his last defense in the court of the Shah, Masoud Rajavi, one of the top leaders of the PMOI, declared: "Since the beginning of the new century, 800 million people in China and 300 million people in USSR have become free."[63] "Towhid" is a central Islamic term meaning the unitary and oneness of Allah. According to Masoud Rajavi, the PMOI combines the Islamic terms "Towhid" and "Nabovat" (prophethood) and regard themselves as the leaders (like prophets) of the movement to create a classless society. The PMOI advocated the abolition of class oppression (capitalism) under the leadership of Rajavi.[64] Under Masoud Rajavi's leadership after the revolution, the PMOI was structured along strict hierarchical lines analogous to the Communist Party of the Soviet Union under Stalin. Interestingly, Rajavi insisted that the main problem with Marxism and materialist worldview was that they were economistic and did not recognize the saliency of leadership. Rajavi argued that Leninism was necessary, and added that the communists still lacked a proper appreciation for the central role and the absolute saliency of leadership.[65]

In the period between February 1979 to mid-1981, the PMOI emerged as one of the largest groups in Iran. The PMOI ideology of combining militant anti-Americanism, anti-imperialism, anti-capitalism, and Islamism matched very well the predominant mood of the time. Both Khomeini and the PMOI were the main beneficiaries of this public mood, which was created in large part due to the Shah's subservience to the US. The predominant public mood for Islamism helped all Islamist groups (fundamentalist, PMOI, LMI, and Bani Sadr) although secular forces (INF, Fadaian, Tudeh) had played a more prominent role in fighting against the Shah's regime. The anti-imperialist mood of the time, helped Khomeini and PMOI to mobilize the masses against the Islamist liberals and others (e.g., secular liberal democrats). The fact that the PMOI had assassinated several Americans in the early 1970s was a major source of popularity for the PMOI which emerged as the most militant anti-American group in the post-revolutionary period.[66] In its official party organ, "Mojahed," the PMOI declared: "The reaction in our era is the world imperialism, and at its head the U.S. imperialism." It added: "Because no humane and peaceful relations is possible between the people and imperialism as the main enemy of the people, then the only correct and revolutionary response for the resolution of this contradiction is a violent and armed struggle against it. Therefore, any dependence or tendency towards imperialism whether political, economic, military, or cultural is reactionary." And the PMOI concluded "any rejection of the necessity of violent struggle against imperialism is reactionary."[67]

From 1985, Rajavi transformed the PMOI from a mass movement into a cult with himself as its guru. Among the weird decrees, Rajavi has ordered many married members to stop conjugal relations, and others to get divorce.[68] In the period February 1979 to mid-1981, the PMOI was a typical authoritarian party, not much different than other Stalinist groups in Iran such as the Fadaian, Paykar, and Tudeh. Hundreds of thousands of the most decent men and women who wanted social justice joined the PMOI in those years and made huge sacrifices in the struggle against the brutal reactionary regime of Ayatollah Khomeini. From 1985, however, under the terrible leadership of Rajavi, the PMOI had been reduced to a strange cult. The PMOI routinely viciously attacks Iran's most respected democratic leaders and human rights advocates who have dared to criticize Rajavi's numerous mistakes and the internal dictatorship in the PMOI. The PMOI's favorite tactic is to slander the democratic opposition leaders as agents of the fundamentalist regime's Intelligence Ministry.

According to Abdol Karim Lahiji, "Massoud Rajavi is Iran's Pol Pot."[69] Mr. Lahiji is Iran's foremost human rights activist and lawyer, and is regarded as one of the most respected Iranian democrats. Mr. Lahiji, Esq., is the Vice President of the International Federation of Human Rights Associations and the President of the Society for the Defense of Human Rights in Iran. He was the lawyer for the PMOI in Tehran between 1979 and 1981. He is a legal advisor on refugees for France's Foreign Ministry.

In the words of Dr. Mohammad Borghei, the PMOI is "totalitarian, power-hungry, revolutionary, slanderer, and cruel." Dr. Borghei is a member of the Iran Liberation Movement, which is a liberal Islamist party.

The following analysis of the PMOI is for the period between 1979 and 1983, when the PMOI was a communist Islamist organization; this analysis does not apply to the PMOI after 1985, when it became a strange cult. On the issues of gender, the analyses presented and the positions taken by the PMOI in the 1979-1983 period are remarkably similar to those of the Marxist-Leninist Fadaian (especially the fraction which came to be known as the Minority).[70] Both the PMOI and Fadaian considered the compulsory veil and the resistance it generated to be a minor question which was being used by the feminists, the bourgeois liberal forces, and the counter-revolutionaries despite the fact that many of the participants were members of their own organizations who had spontaneously joined the demonstrations.[71]

The PMOI, like the fundamentalists, strongly advocate hejab for women. Both the PMOI and the fundamentalists regard the demand of feminist women not to wear the hejab as due to the corrupt imperialist culture of the West. The PMOI issued its declaration on hejab on March 12, 1979. The PMOI declared: "Hejab, as a revolutionary foundation of Islam, is in fact nothing but a social effort for the sake of observance and protection of morality in society; it is without doubt one of the necessities of an all-embracing social, material and spiritual development; and we are sure that our revolutionary sisters and mothers, as they have so far proved in practice, also have observed this necessity and will continue to do so."[72] The only difference between Khomeini and the PMOI was that Khomeini wanted to impose the hejab through violence immediately, and the PMOI wanted to pursue a more gradual process. Even by the year 2,001 the PMOI enforces compulsory hejab on its own members. In other words, if a female member of the PMOI decided not to wear hejab, she will be expelled from the PMOI.

Both the PMOI and the Fadaian-Minority stressed the danger of the women's movement, and attacked the degenerate imperialist culture, while also opposing the violent manner by which the fundamentalists imposed the hejab.[73]

The PMOI's analysis of the inferior position of women is remarkably close to that of Engels, i.e., although gender is mentioned at the theoretical level, in a concrete analysis, class is always the primary explanatory factor. The only difference between the analysis of the PMOI and the analysis by Engels is that the PMOI insert quotations of some of the verses of the Koran in order to justify their otherwise traditional Marxist analysis.[74] The following quotation is from an internal educational and theoretical pamphlet published and distributed in 1979 whose main audience was the members and supporters of the Mojahedin:

> ...*tawhidi* is against any class, racial, national, and sexual discrimination. It cannot, therefore, accept the discrimination between women and men as a holy matter and approve it....
>
> *Particularly today, that is, in the 20th Century and after the emergence of the revolutionary class of workers in the scene of human society, that is, a class that is historically destined to strike the final blow to the exploitation which is the root of all discriminations, the best of opportunities to struggle for the elimination of sexual discriminations have been also provided.*
>
> A glance at the *Qur'an*: It suffices here to mention that both the actual historical examples set out by the true leaders of Islam in connection with the role of women and the verses of the *Qur'an*, are *tawhidi* in their approach to the historical role of women and can never fit within such a discriminatory framework....
>
> 'O mankind. We have created you male and female, and appointed you races and tribes, that you may know one another. Surely the noblest among you in the sight of God is the most godfearing of you. God is all-knowing, all-aware.' (Surah Apartments, Verse 13)
>
> With regard to a correct understanding of the question of piety: piety is a quality that is the expression of the liberation of individuals and society from the individual and social constraints by means of consciousness. It is clear that in the *tawhidi* outlook, where there is the question of measurement of superiorities, there is no place for social, racial and sexual discriminations. And, contrary to polytheistic class societies, if *tawhidi* relations rule over society it will transform social relations in such a way

that the superiorities and competences will be measured practically on the basis of piety and not sexuality, or race or anything else.

Contrary to the historical outlooks based on the acceptance of sexual superiority, and contrary to reactionary perceptions of Islam which pretend that men and women have no similar essence and have been created out of different mould. We must remember that the *Qur'an* emphatically stresses the single origin and mould and equal essence of men and women:

'Mankind, fear your Lord, who created you of a single soul, and from it created its mate, and from the pair of them scattered abroad many men and women....' (Surah Women, Verse 1)

Therefore, *tawhidi outlook believes that discriminations are not the result of differences in human essence but the product of the functions of various class systems....*

Knowledge also teaches us that this society of primitive equality and brotherhood disintegrated at a certain stage of its development. This was partly structural, due to the evolution of technique, increased use of nature and hence emergence of possibility of exploitation. Class antagonism thus emerged out of this unity. This was the beginning of the formation of the class societies that reigned one after the other. At first, this was in the form of slavery, that is, the most barbaric kind of exploitation of man by man. Then big landowners became the rulers of the fate of humanity and, for the maximum extraction of profit from the land, exploited human beings like animals and even bought and sold them together with the land. Finally, capitalism, as the most developed and complex class order, dominated humanity. By way of complex technological tools of the times, capitalism began to exploit human beings so as to fill the purses of capitalists.

With a *tawhidi* view of history, the *Qur'an*, while analyzing the original unity of human society and then touching on the formation of classes, believes that ultimately, class antagonisms will be resolved and tend once more towards unity....

The formation of classes and the role of prophets have been mentioned in a beautiful and concise manner in the *Qur'an*:

'The people were once one nation; the God sent forth the Prophets, good tidings to bear and warning, and He sent down with them the Book with the truth....' (Surah Cow, Verse 213).

...It may be concluded that the capitalist class system, compared with the feudal society, does allow a certain amount of freedom to women and, for the necessities of production, drives them to the field of production. However, these freedoms are granted not in order to confer value on women as members of society but for the expansion of consumption and accumulation of capital: women are thus confined in new fetters that prevent their development in the direction of liberation. Women of our time have rightly realized that for liberation they have no choice but to destroy this last stage of evolution of class society and thus achieve the total negation of exploitation....

For centuries under the domination of capitalism, practically all the oppressive features of capitalist societies are generated. In some industrial countries certain useful aspects of industrial growth, such as the relative participation of women in scientific and educational activities can be observed, but such a phenomenon is rarely found in dependent countries. Instead we find only those aspects of capitalist societies which are solely in the service of the sale of commodities and the entry of women into the labour market.[75] [emphasis mine]

The largest armed opposition group in the post-revolutionary period is the PMOI which set up the National Council of Resistance (NCR). In its "Program of the Provisional Government of the Democratic Islamic Republic of Iran," NCR defends the equality of women.[76] In Article 10, it considers the "duty of the provisional government" to be bringing about "absolute legal equality of women... equal political-economic, and social, equal pay for equal work...."[77] On October 22, 1993, the PMOI declared that a woman, the wife of the PMOI leader, will be the President in the Provisional government that they plan to install after overthrowing the fundamentalists.[78]

In the 1979 to 1984 period, the PMOI was very popular and was able to attract a huge number of men and women from urban lower middle class backgrounds to its rank. From February 1979 until late 1980, the PMOI supported Khomeini. In that period, the PMOI was the most virulently anti-American group in Iran, with "Death to U.S. Imperialism" its main slogan, and printed in large letters in its organ, "Mojahed." The PMOI had assassinated several Americans in the early 1970s, including several assassinations in 1972 and 1973 under the leadership of Ahmad Rezaee and Reza Rezaee, two of PMOI's main heros that are honored today as perfect Islamist leaders of the PMOI.[79] The PMOI strongly supported the taking of American diplomats hostage and harshly criticized those Iranians who wanted to release the Americans.[80] In early 1981, the PMOI supported Bani Sadr, the liberal Islamist president, who was in conflict with Khomeini. The conflict came to a climax on June 1981, when armed struggle was called by the PMOI to overthrow the fundamentalist regime. However, by 1984, it became evident that the armed struggles had failed: and then the PMOI went through a major metamorphosis. Initially, the PMOI dropped its anti-imperialist stance and asked the Western government to help it in its struggle to overthrow the fundamentalist regime. By 1985-86, Masoud Rajavi, the already absolute leader of the PMOI, turned the organization into a cult, where he was praised and regarded to be the equivalent of Prophets Abraham, Jesus, Mohammad, Shia Imam Ali, and Shia Imam Hussein combined.[81] An Ideological Revolution was announced. As part of this transformation into a cult, Maryam Azadanlou the wife of one of the highest ranked members of the PMOI got divorced from him and married Masoud Rajavi. All members of the PMOI had to sign their allegiance to this divorce/marriage as the sign of the liberation of women and the Ideological Revolution. Although the PMOI's transformation into a cult and the total worship of Masoud Rajavi were quite strange, the organization emphasized the prominent role of women as a hallmark of this transformation, which it called the "Ideological Revolution." The role of Ms. Maryam Azadanlou-Rajavi became prominent as a spokesperson for the group.

From about 1985, the PMOI's central slogan became: "Iran Rajavi, Rajavi Iran," which in a totalitarian manner equates a whole country with one person. When the democratic and progressive members of the opposition made the smallest criticisms of Rajavi, the whole PMOI propaganda machinery would commence vicious personal attacks against them and spread false rumors that they were collaborating with the fundamentalist regime's Ministry of Intelligence. In 1987, Rajavi and the PMOI moved to Iraq and started close cooperation with Saddam Hussein in the middle of the Iran-Iraq war. Rajavi's close collaboration with Saddam Hussein while Saddam wanted to take over Iran's territory, including the oil-rich Khuzestan province, as well as Saddam's purposeful targeting of civilian population in the war cost the PMOI dearly in legitimacy. Most Iranians regard the PMOI as traitors who sold Iran's national interests to Saddam Hussein in order to get to power. From then on, the PMOI lost its social base in Iran. However, there continues to be a small but highly organized PMOI organization that fiercely engages in propaganda and activities against the fundamentalist regime and the democratic opposition alike.

Notwithstanding the strange transformation of the PMOI into a totalitarian cult after 1985, what should be clear from this section is that it is possible to be both Islamist and produce ideas and analysis which are similar to Marxist feminist analyses.[82] Therefore, one can conclude that Islam is not a sufficient condition (causal factor) invariably giving rise to anti-feminism. In other words, because an avowed Islamist political party (and one of the three most popular organizations in the 1979-1984 period) is supportive of a gender egalitarian society, Islam is not a sufficient condition for anti-feminism.

Many secular Iranian liberal feminists and socialist feminists have criticized the PMOI for ignoring the obviously explicit patriarchal verses in the Koran, arguing that their interpretations of these verses are not warranted.[83] There is no question that there are many obvious problems with the PMOI's interpretation of Islam.[84] However, the analytically significant point is that the PMOI and their supporters accept these interpretations of Islam as the true Islam.

RADICAL FEMINISM[85]

Radical feminists on a continuum from the most extreme (Shulamith Firestone) to the most moderate (Marilyn Frye) agree on one thing: the belief that sex is the primary contradiction in human society at all times and in all places.[86] All other hierarchies such as class, race, age, and beauty are ramifications of the basic and essential power differential between men and women. In the words of Robin Morgan:

> ...sexism is the root oppression, the one which, until and unless we uproot it, will continue to put forth the branches of racism, class hatred, ageism, competition, ecological disaster, and economic exploitation.[87]

Men are the oppressors and women are the oppressed, period. To emphasize the maleness of oppressive rule, radical feminists label it "phallocracy."[88]

According to radical feminism, this system in which men (in general) have ruled women is called patriarchy. For radical feminists, patriarchy is omnipresent in all societies and at all times. Various forms of male rule are not categorized but lumped together under the term "patriarchy."[89]

Radical feminists tend to be biological determinists. Although Firestone, for example, concurs with the distinction between sex (biological attribute) and gender (socially constructed), her view is nevertheless such that no amount of socialization can make men different. The difference is biologically rooted and cannot be easily remedied. In Firestone's own words:

Let us first try to develop an analysis in which biology it-self—procreation—is at the origin of the dualism. The immediate assumption of the layman that the unequal division of the sexes is 'natural' may be well-founded. We need not immediately look beyond this. Unlike economic class, sex class sprang directly from a biological reality: men and women were created different, and not equally privi-leged....

...The *biological family*—the basic reproductive unit of male/female/infant, in whatever form of social organization—is character-ized by these fundamental—if not immutable--facts....

...These biological contingencies of the human family cannot be covered over with anthropological sophistries. Anyone observing animal mating, reproducing, and caring for their young will have a hard time accepting the cultural relativity line.[90]

...[Feminist] materialism is that view... of history which seeks the ultimate cause and the great moving power of all historic events in the dialectics of sex; the division of society into two distinct biological classes for procreative reproduction; and the struggles of these classes... in changes in the modes of marriage, reproduction, and child care... in the first division of labor based on sex... [and] in the connected development of other physically differentiated classes [castes]... which [develop] into the [economic/cultural] class system.[91]

In an ironical and paradoxical twist, radical feminists and anti-feminists agree on the importance of biological difference between men and women. In a still more puzzling similarity, both seem to argue that women are less rational than men.[92] The difference between radical feminists and anti-feminists is that for radical feminists the norm of irrationality is positive and women's culture is celebrated.

Most radical feminists regard lesbianism as a **politically** chosen decision (i.e., that to be a lesbian is not an inborn sexual preference).[93] Moreover, any heterosexual relationship is regarded as "more or less synonymous with rape, on the grounds that male sexuality is by definition predatory and sadistic."[94] Therefore, *bona fide* feminists have to be lesbians; anything less is a compromise with males. According to Ti-Grace Atkinson, "Feminism is the theory and lesbianism is the practice."[95] Other feminists (non-lesbian) are simply asking "for a better deal" from their men. In a phallocratic system, Frye and Bunch argue, non-submission to male sexual access is a revolutionary act.

The political effect of radical feminists has been negligible in the U.S. They have been effectively marginalized by the mainstream media. Indeed, whenever the mainstream media want to denigrate the feminist movement, they point to radical feminists. The only instance of their partial success in effecting policy has been when they were in alliance with Jerry Falwell's Moral Majority and other Christian fundamentalists; this alliance helped to pass local ordinances banning pornography.[96] By strengthening the coercive arm of the government, ironically, lesbian literature could also be banned, a side effect that according to critics does not seem to dawn on radical feminists.[97] According to some feminists there are "disturbing" similarities between feminists and the "New Right and its fundamentalist ideologues" not only on strategies to ban pornography but also on analysis of sexuality.[98] In the words of Lillian Robinson:

> What is frightening and confusing is the extent to which feminist and reactionary protests have similar targets and apparently seek the same sort of censorship. How, in even the shortest possible run, can feminists be on the same side as the people who, when they are **not** censoring television, are pulling *Our Bodies, Ourselves* off library shelves and calling for a return to the days when Ozzie Nelson knew best?[99]

According to Margaret Simons it was just these problems plus the inherent contradictions within the radical feminist views on female sexuality that ultimately caused their failure to bring about a mass anti-pornography movement.[100]

As far as Iranian politics is concerned, radical feminism as ideological orientation of social movement has been irrelevant. There are various reasons for this: first, fundamentalist Islam is at the helm of the government and has already banned "pornography." Indeed, violators can be lashed, jailed and even executed for possessing, distributing, or producing pornographic video tapes.[101]

Secondly, the family structure and, therefore, the patriarchal relationship are very different in the Middle East. In the U.S. patriarchal privileges are diffused in the nuclear family unit. Women tend to blame themselves for their problems with their husbands; for women to get together and talk about their experiences is consciousness-raising. Women find out that their problem is not personal but political, and political action may therefore follow. On the contrary, in the Middle East, among traditional sectors of the society men and women are segregated in the first place. In mosques women stand in the back and pray behind men. At weddings and other occasions, among the traditional sectors, women are separated from men.[102]

Among the traditional sectors to intermingle with members of the opposite sex (who are not family-related) in public is considered subversive. The reality of second class citizenship for females is well known and well understood by both men and women. Indeed, if a woman finds a husband that is not "chauvinistic" or a "godzilla," she considers herself lucky.[103] According to noted anthropologist Mary Elain Hegland, unlike "American suburban women," the women from the traditional middle class **in villages** are:

> ...engaged in a complicated round of activities concerned with marriage, pregnancy and birth. In these activities as well as in other types of social interaction, women seemed to lead social lives quite independent of their husbands. They were concerned with other women rather than with relations with men.
> ...Their standing in female society was important to them; the respect of other women was gratifying. Some women became important social leaders of their circle of friends, neighbors and relatives and gained satisfaction from the facts that others respected their opinions and awaited their advice before embarking on activities.[104]

Within Middle Eastern cultural milieu, the radical feminist notion of male patriarchy rooted in biology is widely accepted but its solution has not found fertile soil. I know of no Iranian radical feminist group.

SOCIALIST FEMINISM

Socialist feminists—such as Heidi Hartmann, Gayle Rubin, Zillah Eisenstein and Nancy Hartsock—attempt to synthesize various concepts borrowed from Marxism and radical feminism.[105] From Marxism they borrow concepts of class, class struggle, capitalist production, alienation and imperialism; from radical feminism they borrow concepts of patriarchy and sexuality. Socialist feminists attempt to articulate theories and concepts that can explain complex societies in which various hierarchies of class, gender and race create a multi-layered, inegalitarian system.

In her seminal article, "The Unhappy Marriage of Marxism and Feminism: Towards a More Progressive Union," Heidi Hartmann develops a conceptual framework to analyze capitalism and patriarchy. According to Hartmann, Marxism is inadequate in analyzing the women's situation, because its categories are sex-blind. Feminist theory is not historical enough and lacks the sophistication of Marxism in analyzing class oppression. For Hartmann, patriarchy is not simply a psychic structure but has a social and economic basis. In her own words:

> Engels, Zaretsky, and Dalla Costa all fail to analyze the labor process within the family sufficiently. Who benefits from women's labor? Surely capitalists, but also surely men, who as husbands and fathers receive personalized services at home. The content and extent of the services may vary by class or ethnic or racial group, but the fact of their receipt does not. Men have a higher standard of living than women in terms of luxury consumption, leisure time, and personalized services. A materialist approach ought not ignore this crucial point. It follows that men have a material interest in women's continued oppression.[106]

On the inadequacy of Marxism, Hartmann says:

> ...the categories of Marxist analysis, class, reserve army of labor, wage-laborer, do not explain why particular people fill particular places. They give no clues about why **women** are subordinate to **men** inside and outside the family and why it is not the other way around. **Marxist categories, like capital itself, are sex-blind.** The categories of Marxism cannot tell us who will fill the empty places.[107]

Hartmann borrows the concept of patriarchy from radical feminists such as Kate Millett and Shulamith Firestone, refines it and gives us her version:

> We can usefully define patriarchy as a set of social relations between men, which have a material base, and which, though hierarchical, establish or create interdependence and solidarity among men that enable them to dominate women. Though patriarchy is hierarchical and men of different classes, races, or ethnic groups have different places in the patriarchy, they also are united in their shared relationship of dominance over their women; they are dependent on each other to maintain that domination. Hierarchies 'work' at least in part because they create vested interests in the status quo. Those at the higher levels can 'buy off' those at the lower levels by offering them power over those still lower. In the hierarchy of patriarchy, all men, whatever their rank in the

patriarchy, are bought off by being able to control at least some women.[108]

For Hartmann, class, gender and race are hierarchies in society. Capitalists, in order to maintain control and realize the maximum profits, have to bargain with the independent gender system that has existed prior to capitalism and may continue to exist in post-capitalist society. Capitalism is not all-powerful and is very flexible. The development of family wage and child and female labor legislation at the turn of the century was a compromise between patriarchy and capitalism.[109]

Like Hartmann, Zillah Eisenstein argues that the two hierarchies of patriarchy and capitalism are interdependent but "patriarchy (as male supremacy) existed before capitalism, and continues in postcapitalist societies."[110]

For socialist feminists, one cannot *a priori* theorize on the saliency of each of these hierarchies and the interactions among them. The existence, structure and the relative salience of—and the interactions among—these hierarchies should be empirically investigated. In one society at a particular point in time class may be more important than the other two hierarchies; but at another time in the same society or in another society gender or race/ethnicity may be the primary hierarchy. Unlike radical feminists who regard patriarchy to be universal across time and space, socialist feminists attempt to analyze the specifics of the kind of patriarchal structures in existence in a particular place and time.[111] To simply state that all societies are patriarchal is similar to saying that all societies are class-divided.[112] Marxists, among others, have differentiated various kinds of class-divided societies; slavery, feudalism, capitalism, monopoly capitalism, late capitalism, or Asian mode of production are but some examples of different kinds of class societies.

Unlike traditional Marxists (Marxist feminists), socialist feminists strongly support an independent women's movement as a necessity for human liberation. According to Herbert Marcuse:

I believe the Women's Liberation Movement today is perhaps the most important and potentially the most radical political movement that we have, even if the consciousness of this fact has not yet penetrated the Movement as a whole.[113]

For Marcuse, capitalism and patriarchy are both determinants of political struggles, and therefore a separate women's movement is "not only justified, it is necessary."[114] The two oppressions influence each other, even though they have their own dynamics and origins. In Marcuse's own words:

> The [Women's Liberation] Movement originates and operates within patriarchal civilization; it follows that it must be initially discussed in terms of the actual status of women in the male-dominated civilization.

Secondly, the Movement operates within a class society—here is the first problem; women are not a class in the Marxian sense. The male-female relationship cuts across class lines but the immediate needs and potentialities of women are definitely class-conditioned to a high degree. Nevertheless there are good reasons why 'woman' should be discussed as general category versus 'man'. Namely the long historical process in which the social, mental and even physiological characteristics of women developed as different from and contrasting with those of men.[115]

According to Zillah Eisenstein gender is as important as class for analyzing various polities and political outcomes; in her words:

> While a worker is cut off from his/her creative abilities s/he is still potentially a creative being. This contradiction between existence and essence lies, therefore, at the base of the revolutionary proletariat as well as the revolutionary woman. One's class position defines consciousness for Marx, but, if we utilize the revolutionary ontological method, it need not be limited to this. If we wish to say that a woman is defined in terms of her sex as well, patriarchal relations define her consciousness and have implications for her revolutionary potential as a result. By locating revolutionary potential as it reflects conflicts between people's real conditions (existence) and possibilities (essence), we can understand how patriarchal relations inhibit the development of human essence.
>
> ...Marx never questioned the hierarchical sexual ordering of society. He did not see that this further set of relations made species life unavailable to women, and hence that its actualization could not come about through the dismantling of the class system alone.
>
> ...The historical materialist method must be extended to incorporate women's relations to the sexual division of labor and society as producer and reproducer as well as to incorporate the ideological formulation of this relationship.

For socialist feminists, historical materialism is not defined in terms of the relations of production without understanding its connections to the relations that arise from woman's sexuality—relations of reproduction.[116]

The only Iranian political party to have been associated with socialist feminism was the short-lived United Left Council (ULC), which was a democratic socialist Marxist party.[117] This party took the position that an independent women's movement was necessary to advance women's rights and that the leftist forces should defend women's rights from fundamentalist attacks. In other words, a cross-class alliance of women around gender issues is neither reactionary nor bourgeois but rather a possible ally in the struggle against the fundamentalists and a necessity in the democratic and progressive transformations of Iranian polity. Although the ULC had little immediate impact on the politics of Iran in the early 1980s, it had a tremendous influence on the thinking of the Iranian left thereafter.[118] In an article entitled, "The Necessity of Independence in Women's Struggles," published in its organ *Payam Azadi*, the ULC stated:

> Attention to the pervasive question of inequality between men and women should not be focused solely on class. The situation of women of our country is not the result of [capitalist economic] exploitation alone but it is also the result of a history of centuries of inequality. The women of our society are confronted by essences of the old and inherited oppressions as well as by the rule of religious reactionaries from the Middle Ages [referring to the ruling fundamentalists]. *Pedarsalary* [Patriarchal] traditions, rules and cultural remnants from past centuries confront women which make the inequalities originating from our current social system even worse, and together they have increased the pressures of inequality in all areas of life. One could not look at the complex question of inequality between men and women in static, ahistorical and class-reductionist ways. We should not forget that our society is facing a situation which is not caused solely by current [economic] exploitative relations but also by traditional oppression, ignorance and old inequalities. Women who have been oppressed by the old patriarchal oppression in our society endure double oppression.
>
> Women in our society are confronted by a constellation of devastating pressures that are the remnants of our history and distant past. It is no wonder then that in the face of such heavy oppression, women are intimidated into....
>
> In our view concerning the question of women, one cannot only limit oneself to class analysis because the women's question as a social whole,

regardless of the class bases of women, is on its own a social-historical problem. During the history of our country women, regardless of which [economic] class position they belong to, simply because they are women, have been considered as second-class creatures, treated as minors....

In today's Iran, although class oppression takes a heavy toll on the shoulders of toiling women, the patriarchal and anti-civic regime of the mullahs has stamped a humiliating inferiority on the forehead of the majority of all women. Therefore, we realize that the slogan against the class oppression of toiling women is not adequate to the various dimensions of the problem. The question of women's liberation from the chains of decaying patriarchal relations tears asunder all boundaries of class and strata and demands liberation in the true sense of the term for women. We do not demand only the abolition of the class oppression of toiling women but go further and demand the liberation of women in our society from all the rotting and decaying aspects which for centuries have put down women. In the same vein that we do not analyze the women's question solely on the basis of class, we also do not look at the women's movement in relation to class alone.... For us, the women's movement, regardless of the class background of its participants, is a social movement; it is an independent movement with its own essence and belongs to women as a social whole; and its march towards liberation is propelled by the historical.... It is obvious that based on our stated views we do not regard class-based organizations [i.e., solely proletarian women's groups] which are organized by this or that party to be an answer to the necessities of the women's movement. The question of women is a question for all women, and the women's movement belongs to all women and the women's organization also should be an organization for all women.

Perhaps choosing March 8th as Women's Day, which celebrates the first protests by working class women that focuses attention on the dual oppressions of women in a capitalist society is not appropriate for those oppressors who plan to force and incarcerate women in the kitchen and the bedroom [referring to Khomeini who demanded that the birthday of Fatima, the Prophet's daughter, replace March 8th as Women's Day].

The conscious struggles of Iranian women have shown that... the rulers of yesterday and today [the Pahlavi and the Islamic Republic regimes] cannot dampen the permanent and indefatigable struggles of the oppressed women of Iran on the two fronts of struggles: struggle against [class] exploitation and struggle against patriarchal reactionary cultural values.

In the end we reiterate that the necessary condition of victory in this historical struggle for the liberation of women is in the emergence, growth and extension of an independent women's movement.[119]

The existence of the ULC in addition to the existence of other groups associated with Marxist feminism (Fadaian) and liberal feminism (National Front) demonstrates that a significant proportion of Iranian people and the politically involved Iranians embraced a gender equal worldview, therefore, disproving the notion that Islam as a civilization, produces people and values that are invariably anti-feminist.

CONCLUSION

It is of prime analytical significance that Iranian society was able to produce so many political parties which were emphatically feminist and that so many Iranian women valiantly and consistently resisted Islamic fundamentalism because of its gender policies. The fact that the fundamentalists won the struggle in 1981 simply indicates that at that particular juncture, anti-feminist forces were more powerful than the progressive forces. Insofar as the struggle against the Islamic Republic of Iran is not completed, the jury on Iran's women's and feminist movements is still out.

However, thanks to the misogynist policies of Ayatollah Khomeini and his fundamentalist successors, no country possesses a generation of women so aware of their trampled-upon rights and so self-consciously feminist. I am confidant that the post-fundamentalist regime in Iran will have no choice but to grant full legal equality to women. I would not be surprised to see the post-fundamentalist regime implement one of the world's most extensive social policies allowing women *de facto* equality. Time will tell!

In the previous chapter I demonstrated that Islamic fundamentalism is obviously misogynist and in this chapter I demonstrated that Islam (as an ideology or as a civilization) is neither a necessary condition nor a sufficient condition for anti-feminism. In the next chapters I attempt to show that Islam is a contributing factor to anti-feminism.

Figure 3-1: Political Ideologies

	Mode of Production	Theorist	Religious Views	Values	Human Nature	Justice
Classical Conservatism	antiquity, feudalism, pastoralism, Asiatic mode of production	Plato	Medieval Catholic Church: "It is easier for the camel to go through the eye of a needle than a rich man to go to heaven." Medieval Islam	blind loyalty, order, harmony, obedience, stability, social inequality, natural aristocracy, wisdom of the past.	Different people have different natures. Gold: guardians/ philosopher-kind Silver: auxiliaries/ soldiers/police Brass: artisans, farmers, etc.	Each individual ought to do what he or she is supposed to do; organic view of society.
Classical Liberalism	Capitalism	John Locke Adam Smith J.S. Mill	Protestantism: "God helps those who help themselves."	democracy, individual rights and liberties, utilitarianism. Conflict is natural to human society.	acquisitive, competitive, self-interested, individualist	fair procedures, equality of opportunity
Classical Socialism	"The coming of Socialism"	Karl Marx, F. Engles	Atheism: Religion is the answer for anxieties and insecurities of life and God is the projection of human values. "A farmer who has access to piped water need not pray for rain."	cooperation, community, economic security. "Criticize everything regardless of whom it may offend." Conflicts and contradictions are what propels society forward.	Human nature changes according to the economic structure of society.	equality, equality of end result. "From each according to his abilities to each according to his needs."

Figure 3-2: Ideological Roots of Theories of Gender

{ Fascism
Classical Conservatism - {   - - - - - - - - - -{ Anti-feminism
{ Religious Fundamentalism

{ Modern Conservatism
Classical Liberalism - - -{
{ Modern Liberalism - - - - - - - - { Liberal Feminism

{ Social Democracy
{ Leninism - - - - - - - - - - - - - { Marxist Feminism
Classical Socialism - - - - {
{ Council Communism
{ Modern New Left - - - - - - { Socialist Feminism

- - - - - - - - - - -{ Radical Feminism

CHAPTER 4

THE KORAN AND PATRIARCHY

In this chapter I intend to argue that Islam is a contributing factor for the anti-feminist policies pursued by the fundamentalists in post revolutionary Iran. In order to do so I demonstrate that there are many important tenets of Islam which are clearly and explicitly anti-feminist and undermine a gender egalitarian society. Those individuals and groups who so wish could draw upon these anti-feminist aspects of Islam to bolster their position thus undermining the position of forces struggling for gender egalitarianism. In essence anti-feminist forces could call upon the anti-feminist tenets of Islam to give legitimacy to their demands. This compels the Islamists who are not anti-feminist to take defensive positions which are very weak. The politically attentive public is then forced into the dichotomy of either abandoning their religious precepts if they wish to remain feminist, or abandoning their feminist demands in the face of the anti-feminists' legitimate Islamic arguments.

Of course many people can live with some degree of logical inconsistency; however, when there are a whole host of conflicts around these issues, one cannot but confront this dilemma. As long as the government is in the hands of secular leaders with nominal allegiance to Islam, these issues remain simmering beneath the surface. However, when Islamic fundamentalists take power, the population is forced to make the unpleasant choice between anti-feminist religious beliefs on the one hand or gender egalitarian proclivities on the other hand. In this section I discuss the anti-feminist tenets and aspects of Islam and the Shariah.

The *Shariah*, or Islamic law, is comprised of rules which one may find in: (1) the Koran (which is regarded to be the literal word of God revealed to the Prophet by the angel Gabriel); (2) the *Hadith* (for Sunnis, the words and deeds of the Prophet Mohammed, and for Shias the words and deeds of the Prophet Mohammad and the 12 Imams); (3) *qiyas*, or analogical reasoning, where a new regulation may be deduced based on analogies of already accepted rules (e.g., opium may be prohibited because it has the same qualities as alcoholic beverages although there is no such prohibition on opium in the Koran or Hadith); and (4) the *ijma*, or the consensus of the theological scholars.

I will demonstrate that unequal treatment and patriarchal laws are traced to the letter of the Koran in areas of polygyny, sexual access to female slaves, divorce, inheritance and testimony. These patriarchal laws are not the creations of commentators who have somehow injected their own patriarchal beliefs into a Koran and God who believe that men and women are equal.

FEMALES' OBEDIENCE AND
INFERIORITY TO MALES

One can point to the following passage in the Koran, which explicitly sanctions patriarchal domination:

> Men are the maintainers of [or have authority over] women because Allah has made some of them to excel others and because they spend out of their property; the good women are therefore obedient, guarding the unseen as Allah has guarded; and (as to) those on whose part you fear desertion, admonish them, and leave them alone in the sleeping-places and beat them; then if they obey you, do not seek a way against them; surely Allah is High, Great.[1]

Although this verse is unambiguous I will quote a commentary by Ayatollah Agha Haji Mirza Mahdi Pooya Yazdi who is a conventional high-ranking cleric. There is no controversy on this verse and the following commentary should make clear that anti-feminism is anchored in the letter and interpretation of the Koran. According to Ayatollah Pooya Yazdi:

However much it may be resented by the selfish and the false regard to womankind in the name of modern chivalry, man is unquestionably superior, not only in physique but also in his intellect and natural dominance in many respects of the native endowments, over a woman. The native endowments of strength in man and beauty in a woman respectively decide this universally acknowledged factor of man's superiority over a woman. The beauty and the delicacy endowed in a woman needs protection and protection can come only from strength which is given to man. Hence a husband is to domineer over his wife and the wife in regard for the protection and the other benefits bestowed upon her by her husband has naturally to be subordinate and obedient to him. Undoubtedly there are qualities which are the essential requisites to fit a being to maintain and control certain things and situations. Owing to the differences in the quality and the quantity of the native endowments in man and a woman viz. the various faculties of the Mind, Temperaments, Sensibilities, Will-power, Emotions, Courage and the various other personality traits, man is naturally more fitted to rule the family and the matters of society, to solve the problems of the nation and the politics of the world, than a woman. None can deny the functions of nature respectively assigned in the two sexes which determine those differences that justify and establish man, all the world over, to be the protector and the maintainer of his wife. A woman is always justly proud of the strength, power and the authority of her husband while the man rejoices and enjoys the beauty, modesty and dutifulness of his wife, and this is only a relative superiority based upon mutual relations and correct understanding of the truth about the personal position of each one in relation to the other.[2]

In this verse the Koran affirm patriarchy as divine. The reason the Koran gives is that men are biologically endowed with superior qualities. The commentators have elaborated on the qualities which makes men superior to women. Among these one finds physical strength, intellect and rationality. The Koran also mentions wealth as a justification for men's authority over women. Women are told by the Koran to be obedient. If women are disobedient, the Koran urges men first to admonish them. If that fails, men are urged to refrain from having sex with them. If that fails, then the Koran urges men to beat their wives. And finally to divorce them.

In verse 38:44, Allah tells the Prophet Job to beat up his wife as he has made an oath to do so. The verse reads: "And take in your hand a green branch and beat her with is and do not break your oat; surely We found him patient; most excellent the servant! Surely he was frequent in returning to (to Allah)." In his commentary on this verse, Ayatollah Pooya Yazdi explains: "Job had taken an oath that he would punish his wife for listening to Satan, with a hundred stripes. To be true to his solemn commitment in God's holy name, Job was commanded by God to strike her with a bundle of hundred sticks to fulfil the oath."[3]

POLYGYNY

In several verses, the Koran explicitly allows polygyny but not polyandry.[4] It has become commonplace to argue that the Koran has limited the number of wives to four citing Surah 4, Verse 3. However, this verse specifically refers to orphans put in charge of a male guardian. This guardian of the orphans is encouraged to marry "two and three and four" of these orphans. If my understanding is correct, the commentators have actually restricted the number of wives to four. In other words, the Islam of the Koran and the Prophet gave males the right to have unlimited number of wives, and it was the commentators who actually reduced these rights.

Because the deeds of the Prophet Mohammad and the Shia Imams are part of the Shariah, their deeds cannot be considered as contradicting the Shariah. We know that the Prophet Mohammad had more than 13 wives, at least three concubines (female sex-slaves) and three other women "who gave themselves to the Prophet." The Prophet's grandson and the Second Shia Imam, Hassan Ibn Ali, is reported to have had as many as 200 wives. Shia sources, however, report that 70 to 300 women had sexual relations with Imam Hassan; some were permanent wives, others sigheh, and still others concubines (or sex-slaves). It appears that the Koran nowhere states limits on how many women a man can marry. Moreover, the marital and sexual lives of the Prophet and other major leaders seem to indicate this.

Popular perception notwithstanding, there are no Biblical prohibitions against polygyny either. Many Biblical Prophets, including David and Solomon, were polygynist. In 1 Kings 11:3 in the Old Testament, the Bible writes that King Solomon "had seven hundred wives of royal birth and three hundred concubines." David is believed to have had ninety nine wives. Jewish prohibition against polygyny in the twentieth century is not anchored in the Bible. Some Christian sects, notably the Church of Christ of Later-day Saints (Mormons), had also allowed polygyny. One of their early Prophets had several dozen wives.

MALE SEXUAL ACCESS TO HIS
FEMALE SLAVES

The Koran explicitly allows a male sexual access to his female slaves or what the Koran calls "what your right hand possesses."[5] The Arabic words "al-nesa al-malakat" which the Koran uses most often literally mean "a woman which is one's property" or "female slave." In most English translations of the Koran, terms such as "what your right hand possesses," "female slaves," "girl-slaves," or "concubine" are used.

In Surah 4, Verse 24, the Koran forbids men to have sexual relations with already-married women except to married female slaves or married female war booties. "Forbidden to you" (4: 23) are "...all married women except those whom your right hand possess..." (4: 24). Ali Dashti gives the following explanation:

A female slave acquired by purchase or captured in war may be taken in marriage without moral compunction or legal impediment even though she already has a husband. An explanation is given in a report quoted by Ebn Sa'd: "Some female captives fell into our hands in the fighting at Awtas (near Honayn), and as they had husbands, we refrained from intercourse with them and consulted the Prophet. Then came the revelation of the words.... Possession of those captives was thus made lawful for us."

In Surah 33, Verse 50, the Koran specifies women that the Prophet and the believers can have conjugal relations with in the following words:

O Prophet! surely We have made lawful to you your wives whom you have given their dowries, and those whom your right hand possesses out of those whom Allah had given to you as prisoners of war, and ... and a believing woman if she gave herself to the Prophet, ... specially for you, not for the (rest of) believers; We know what We have ordained for them concerning their wives and those whom their right hands possess...

Indeed, the Prophet Mohammad himself owned several such sex-slaves. Maria the Copt (Christian) and Rayhana (Jewish) were among the Prophet's sex-slaves or concubines. According to Ali Dashti:

Mariya the Copt, a slave-girl who was sent from Egypt as a gift to the Prophet. She bore him a son, Ebrahim, who died in infancy.

Reyhana, like Mariya the Copt, fell into the Qor'anic category of "those whom your right hands have acquired" i.e. she was a slave-girl with whom contractual marriage was unnecessary but concubinage was permissible. She was one of the captives from the Jewish Banu Qorayza and the Prophet's share of the booty taken from that tribe. She was unwilling to profess Islam and enter into a contractual marriage with the Prophet, preferring to retain the status of a slave in his house.[6]

The following passage in the Koran was "revealed" when apparently some of the Prophet's wives were unhappy with his ever-growing number of wives. At that time the Prophet had nine wives and a number of slave-girls. The Koran says:

O Prophet, we have made lawful to you the wives to whom you have granted dowries and the slave-girls whom Allah has given you as booty.... We will know the duties we have imposed on the faithful concerning their wives and slave-girls.... You may put off any of your wives you please and take to your bed any of them you please. Nor is it unlawful for you to receive any of those whom you temporarily set aside. That is more proper, so that they may be contented and not vexed, and may all be pleased with what you give them. It shall be unlawful for you to take more wives or to change your present wives for other women, though their beauty please you, except where slave-girls are concerned....[7]

Although slavery was abolished in the Middle East in the twentieth century, there are still a few fundamentalist activists who call for a return of sex-slaves or concubinage as a remedy for prostitution and venereal diseases. According to Nazih Ayubi, who is one of the foremost scholars of the Middle East:

A few of the Islamists are so out of touch with realities that they still speak—in the present tense—of the man's right to have intercourse with his female slaves.* Even the renowned contemporary Syrian Islamist Sa'id Hawwa subscribes to this fantasy: 'What would a man whose lust has been aroused do? He has no option of course except to marry or possess a female slave [ama]!'***.[8]

DIVORCE

In verses dealing with divorce in the Koran, God speaks directly to men, telling them the rules on divorce.[9] In Surah 2, Verse 229, the Koran simply tells males: "Divorce may be (pronounced) twice." The absolute right of males to unilaterally divorce women (even without their knowledge), while women have to go to a religious judge to have their husband divorced is clearly anchored in the Koranic verses. In other words, the specific and complex rules and regulations which have been created by the commentators are based on the Koran which simply gives males the right to divorce their wives but does not grant such rights to women. In Surah 2, Verses 231 and 232 the Koran says: "And when you divorce women and they..." and "And when you have divorced women and they..." it is males who are addressed and given the right to divorce their wives. No such passage in which the Koran speaks to women exists. To the extent that there are divorce rights for women in Islam, these rights have been created by the commentators based on two verses in the Koran that are at best ambiguous.[10]

In Surah 2, Verse 228, the Koran, explicitly states that:

And the divorced women should keep themselves in waiting for three courses [menstrual cycles]; and it is not lawful for them that they should conceal what Allah has created in their wombs, if they believe in Allah and the last day; and their husbands have a better right to take them back in the meanwhile if they wish for reconciliation; ...and **the men are a step above women.**[11]

INHERITANCE

The fact that women receive one-half the inheritance that men receive is not the innovation of alleged conservative commentators who distorted the alleged original egalitarian ethos of the Prophet and the Koran but is explicitly stated in the Koran. In Sura 4, Verse 11, the Koran states: "Allah enjoins you concerning your children: The male shall have the equal of the portion of two females..." In the following verse the Koran states:

And you [the male] shall have half of what your wives leave if they have no child, but if they have a child, then you shall have a fourth of what the leave...; and they [females] shall have the fourth of what you leave if you have no child, but if you have a child then they shall have the eighth of what you leave...(Surah 4, Verse 12).[12]

TESTIMONY

Like the discrimination in inheritance rights, it is the Koran itself that explicitly states that women's testimony at courts are valued less than those of men. In Surah 2, Verse 282, the Koran states:

> ...and call in to witness from among your men two witnesses; but if there are not two men, then one man and two women from among those whom you choose to be witnesses...

It is clear from this verse that the discrimination against women is neither the creation of the medieval "conservative" commentators, nor of the traditional clerics nor of the contemporary fundamentalists. The call by liberal Islamists and communist Islamists for juridical equality at the courts of law is not grounded in the Koran.

DID ISLAM BRING ABOUT IMPROVEMENT
IN THE STATUS OF WOMEN?

In the 1980s and 1990s a debate began among feminists and scholars on the question of whether it is Islam per se or the fundamentalist variety which is in essence anti-feminist.[13] The conventional view expressed by Muslims (of all stripes including governments, liberal Islamists, communist Islamists and fundamentalists) is that prior to the rise of Islam, the status of women in Arabia was extremely low and that the Prophet Mohammad and Islam improved women's position.

However, recent social scientific research by some feminists from the Middle East demystify what they regard as propaganda. They argue that before the rise of Islam, the position of women was better.[14] First, contrary to popular, Islamic, and Islamist views, a woman's right to own property, transact business and manage trade is not a right granted by Islam but a right which existed in pre-Islamic Arabia. For example, the Prophet Mohammad's first wife, Khadijeh, was one of the richest merchants in Mecca. Khadijeh's wealth was accumulated **prior to** the invention of Islam, not after it.[15] Khadijeh was not the only influential and successful Arab woman in business. Scholars maintain that, "There were many others in trade, such as the mother of Abu-Jahal who traded in perfumery, and Hind the wife of Abu-Sofyan who traded with Syrians."[16]

Second, in Islam the father's permission is necessary for the marriage of his daughters. From what we know, in pre-Islamic Arabia women seem to have had the power to ask for marriage and many did ask not only for marriage but also for sexual intercourse.[17] For example, it was the wealthy Khadijeh, who was 15 years older than Mohammed, who asked Mohammed to marry her.[18] According to authentic Hadith, the first time Khadijeh asked Mohammad to marry her, Mohammad refused. The second time Khadijeh asked, Mohammad agreed to marry her.[19]

Even more important is another authentic Hadith which conveys the story of the day the Prophet was conceived. According to this Hadith, the Prophet's father was on his way to the home of the Prophet's mother; a woman asked Mohammad's father to have intercourse with her. Mohammad's father said that he was on his way to another place. The next day (after Mohammad was conceived) when Mohammad's father was on his way back he sees the same woman and tells her that he is now free and can engage in intercourse. The woman had changed her mind and tells him that there was something special about him the day before which was absent now. The purpose of this Hadith is to establish the divine intent and plan in Mohammad's conception. However, it illustrates that: (1) in pre-Islamic Arabia, women had the right to ask for intercourse; and (2) in the early post-Islamic era, the memory of sexually assertive women was strong enough to make such a story plausible and believable.[20]

Third, the scholarly consensus is that in pre-Islamic Arabia, some women possessed sexual self-determination. There appear to have been two major trends or kinds of unions between men and women. In one kind, the woman remained with her tribe and the children belonged to her and her tribe. There were various forms of this marriage, some of which allowed the woman more than one husband. The second kind involved men who had either purchased their women or had captured them as booty in war; in this kind, the man owned the children and the woman. Mohammad condemned and forbade the first kind as *zina* (adultery, fornication) and instituted the second kind as the only legitimate form of marriage.[21] Gertrude Stern's research indicates that in pre-Islamic Arabia there was no polygyny in the sense of one man maintaining more than one woman in one location (that form of polygyny seems to have started at the same time as the rise of Islam).[22]

Both traditional Ulama and fundamentalists argue that polygyny is benign because it is of divine origins. However, it appears that the Prophet did not wish it for his own daughters, particularly his favorite daughter, Fatima who was married to Ali. Fatima, whom the Shias consider to be sinless and a model woman, is described in Sunni sources with negative characteristics. It is said that she was always sick and constantly bickered with Ali who became the Fourth Caliph and First Shia Imam.[23] When Ali decided to marry a second wife, the Prophet adamantly opposed him and said: "I will not allow Ali Ibn Abi Talib and I repeat, I will not allow Ali to marry another woman except if he divorces my daughter. She is part of me, and what harms her, harms me."[24] If the institution of polygyny is benign, why did the Prophet consider it harmful to his favorite daughter? Ali was not allowed to marry another woman until Fatima's death. After the deaths of the Prophet Mohammad and Fatima, Imam Ali married numerous wives.[25] From Ali's will we could deduce that after Fatima's death he owned several concubines in addition to his regular wives. Imam Ali writes in his will:

> Those female slaves who live in my house and may be pregnant, if they deliver after me, they are also due a share of my wealth, as their child is also my child and will be entitled to a legitimate share. But if a pregnant slave delivers and her child dies, then she is free to go.[26]

Fourth, the fact that in pre-Islamic Arabia there existed goddess worship, a few matriarchal tribes, and polyandry (in a few tribes), as well as the fact that many women actively participated in battles with swords and daggers, indicates the independent and powerful position of women relative to that in the Islamic period, which strengthened patriarchal tendencies and relations.[27]

Fifth, in pre-Islamic Arabia as well as during the earliest Islamic era, women had the right and the effective power to divorce, a right and power which was radically restricted if not completely destroyed afterwards. Indeed, three of the Prophet's own wives divorced him and his granddaughter, Sakina Bint al-Hussein, "married often and left husbands she did not like."[28]

Sixth, in at least one very significant aspect, the commentaries which were written after the Prophet Muhammad's life, restricted the number of wives a man could have. All the four Sunni schools of law and the Shias restrict males to only four permanent wives (at any one time). As already discussed the Prophet had 13 or 17 wives and several concubines. If the Prophet's deeds constitute the Shariah, then the commentaries restriction to only four wives is a real advance for women.

Fatima Mernissi cites the story of Amina, the Prophet's great-grand-daughter, to illustrate that in the immediate post-Islamic era women understood that their position and status had suffered compared to pre-Islamic times. When Amina was asked why she was so funny and humorous while her sister, Fatima, was so deadly serious, Amina quipped: "It is because she [Fatima] was named after her Muslim grandmother [Fatima is the daughter of the Prophet] while I was named after my pagan great-great-grandmother, who died before Islam's arrival. [Amina is the mother of the Prophet.]."[29]

From the discussion in this section we can reach the following four conclusions. First, the status of women deteriorated with the rise of Islam. This may or may not be attributable to Islam but rather to the rise of urbanism and commerce in Arabia, which entailed the rise of both Islam and a deterioration of women's position. In other words, certain elements of Islam are a reflection of rising patriarchal relations. Second, the Koran contains many passages that are explicitly patriarchal and advocate discriminatory laws against women.[30] Third, the position of women became progressively worse as time went on. In other words, the position of women became far worse in later times than during the early Islamic period. Fourth, the Koran and the Hadith which reflect the earliest Islamic texts contain passages which may be interpreted to the benefit of women against the traditionalists and fundamentalists who rely more heavily on the commentaries which are more misogynist. Fifth, Islamic fundamentalism is the most anti-feminist version of Islam and presents a threat to the position of women in general and to the position of educated women in particular.[31]

CONCLUSION

In chapter Three I demonstrated that there are liberal Islamist, communist Islamist and secular (but privately devout) political parties and leaders in Iranian polity that also advocate gender equality, therefore, Islam cannot be regarded as a sufficient factor causing anti-feminism. In chapter Two, I demonstrated that fundamentalists implemented *de jure* and *de facto* policies against female equality. In this chapter I demonstrated that the Koran contains verses which are explicitly patriarchal and discriminate against women. Islamic fundamentalists who are anti-feminist can make use of these verses to bolster their position and undermine those who advocate gender equal policies. In this respect Islam may be understood as a contributing factor to gender inequality.

CHAPTER 5

FUNDAMENTALIST PURITANISM
AND ISLAM

After assuming power, Khomeini and his fundamentalist followers instituted sexually puritanical rules and regulations. The fundamentalists established draconian gender segregation in both public and private areas. For example, the Islamic Revolutionary Guards began a practice of interrogating couples in parks, on streets or other public areas. The couple would be arrested if they could not prove that they were related either through blood or marriage. The couple faced lashes, imprisonment and their parents were required to come and take them from the authorities. Vice squads invaded homes in which they suspected men and women were attending parties in which they might be dancing together.

The extreme puritanism of the fundamentalists has gone to truly bizarre extremes. In one case, a female university student at the Tehran University's Department of Foreign Languages was suspended for one academic year because she sat down in a chair which a male student had just vacated. The monitor in the classroom reasoned that the chair was still warm and the female should not have chosen that seat. In another case, in the same department, both a male and a female student were suspended for one semester because the male student had given the female student a video tape to translate. Although the transaction was found to be legitimate and school-related, the administration did not reverse the decision by the monitor who wanted the students suspended for exchanging the tapes directly.[1]

The fundamentalists claim that their puritanical measures are the implementation of Islamic injunctions. In this chapter I argue that the extreme sexual puritanism of the fundamentalists is a radical departure from sexual mores as embodied in the life of the Prophet Mohammad, in Islam and in "historical Shiism."[2] I demonstrate that the ultra-puritanical practices of Islamic fundamentalists in Iran have very little in common with many of the practices of the Prophet and Islam in general and the Shia sect in particular.

SEXUAL PURITANISM AND THE PROPHET MOHAMMAD

The Prophet Mohammed is reputed to have had at least 13 permanent wives and a number of sexual concubines (in the words of Fatima Mernissi, the concubines were the most beautiful women from the defeated Jewish and Christian tribes) as well as four women who "gave themselves to the Prophet."[3] According to Ali Dashti:

> Omm Sharik, of the Daws tribe, was one of four women who gave themselves to the Prophet. In addition to the contractual wives and concubines, there were some women in the Prophet's harem who fell into this category.... Concubinage with slave-women is permissible to Muslims if the woman's husband was a polytheist or other unbeliever. For the Prophet only, marriage to a woman who gave herself was permitted by the last part of verse 49 of sura 33 (ol-Ahzab). The other three women who gave themselves to the Prophet were Maymuna, Zaynab, and Khawla.
>
> Omm Sharik's gift of herself disturbed A'esha, because Omm Sharik was so beautiful that the Prophet immediately accepted the gift. In extreme jealousy and indignation, A'esha reportedly said, "I wonder what a woman who gives herself to a man is worth." The incident is cited as the occasion of the revelation of the last part of verse 49, which sanctioned Omm Sharik's gift and the Prophet's acceptance. On hearing this, A'esha was reportedly so impertinent as to say, "I see that your Lord is quick to grant your wishes."[4]

One should distinguish two quite different periods in the Prophet's marital life. The first period includes his marriage to Khadijeh the wealthy merchant which lasted for 25 years until her death. From what is known, this marriage, which was Mohammad's first marriage, was monogamous and all of the Prophet's children are from this marriage (except for Ibrahim the son, who died in infancy, born to a concubine called Maria the Copt). The second period begins with the death of Khadijeh and spans the last 12 years of the Prophet's life from age of 50 to 62 years. During this time Mohammad—who was not only a prophet but the powerful leader of much of the Arabian peninsula—married at least 12 women and acquired an unknown number of concubines (we are certain of at least three). According to Hojatolislam Abbas Abbasi, a member of the Fourth Majles from Bandar Abbas, the Prophet Mohammad kept eight wives in one house.[5]

Some of these wives were chosen by the Prophet in order to create and maintain alliances between himself and the various tribes. However, many of his wives were chosen solely because of their beauty, which ran counter to one of the Prophet's own sayings. A Hadith relates: "The Prophet said that the woman can be married for her religion [Muslim faith], for her fortune, or her beauty. Be motivated in your choice by her religion."[6] However, when a Jewish tribe was defeated and their women taken as booty, upon hearing the news about the "incomparable beauty" of one of the women named Safiya who had been allotted to a soldier called Dahia (as was the custom among Islamic as well as pre-Islamic raiding teams), the Prophet sent for Dahia and paid him Safiya's price, freed her and married her.[7]

Rayhana Bint Zayd is another well known "beautiful woman" who was captured when her Jewish tribe was defeated; however, there is some controversy over whether she became a concubine or a wife; what is not controversial is that she served absolutely no purpose in alliance politics and the Prophet had chosen her solely for her beauty.[8] There were many other examples of women whom the Prophet chose solely or primarily because of their beauty; among these one may include Maria the Copt, Zainab Bint Jahsh who was the wife of his adopted son Zayd, Juwariya Bint al-Harith and Dubaa Bint Amr.[9]

In pre-Islamic Arabia at least 22 different kinds of marriage existed and as mentioned in the previous chapter historical evidence strongly suggests that women could and did ask men for sexual relations.[10] In such a milieu, some of the Prophet Mohammad's sexual relations raised eyebrows. One such incident was his decision to marry his adopted son's wife, apparently after seeing her half-dressed.[11] In Arabia, adopted children were treated as biological children and their spouses were considered off limits for sexual attraction. In order to sooth the outraged sensibilities of the Islamic umma (community), according to Islamic beliefs, God sent several revelations which became verses in the Koran.[12] All these verses are in the very important Surah 33. In Surah 33, Verses 4 and 5, the Koran reverses traditional Arab custom and rule, and declares that adopted sons have no legal or moral relationship to adoptive fathers. In Surah 33, Verse 37 God directly informs Mohammad that his marriage to the wife of his adopted son Zaid (also spelled Zayd) is divine, and in other verses God threatens anyone who mistrusts the Prophet with hell and violence.[13] Verse 37 of Surah 33 states:

> ...But when Zaid had accomplished his want of her, We gave her to you as a wife, so that there should be no difficulty for the believers in respect of the wives of their adopted sons, when they have accomplished their want of them; and Allah's command shall be performed.[14]

In perhaps one of the most embarrassing episodes in the Prophet's life, he was caught violating a Koranic dictum and his own statement. The Koran requires that a polygamous man treat all his wives equally.[15] This meant that the husband should follow a strict rotation system in which each wife (and concubine?) would sleep with the husband on her day. The Prophet was particularly attracted to a concubine called Maria the Copt (who was a Christian and was a gift from Egypt). Maria was considered to be a "famous beauty" which had made the Prophet's other wives jealous. Ayesha recounted that:

> I never was as jealous as I was of Maria. That is because she was a very beautiful, curly-haired woman. The Prophet was very attracted to her. In the beginning, she was living near us and the Prophet spent entire days and nights with her until we protested and she became frightened.[16]

Hafsa, one of the Prophet's wives, caught the Prophet having intercourse with Maria in Safiya's room and on Safiya's day to have the Prophet. The Prophet had sent Safiya to relay a message to Umar in order to have her out of the room for a while. Umar, realizing that the Prophet wanted Safiya out for a while, kept her busy. The Prophet made a secret agreement with Hafsa; in exchange for Hafsa's silence, the Prophet agreed not to touch Maria ever again. However, Hafsa broke her promise and conveyed to Safiya and Ayesha that the Prophet had violated the rules. Safiya angrily fulminated, "O Prophet of God, in my room and on my day!"[17] Then, according to Islamic belief, God sent revelations ordering the

Prophet to resume his relations with Maria[18] and threatened Safiya and Ayesha telling them that if they did not cease their protests, Allah would replace them with wives who were "better than you, submissive, faithful, obedient, penitent, adorers, fasters, widows and virgins."[19] These revelations became the entire Surah 66 (Verses 1-12). Moreover, this Surah threatened Safiya and Ayesha with hell and the same fate which befell the disobedient wives of Prophets Nuh (Noah) and Lut (Lot).[20]

In another incident, apparently in response to complaints from his wives (especially Ayesha, the Prophet's favorite wife whom he married when she was 9-years-old and had not reached 18 prior to his death) that the Prophet was marrying too many women and not treating them equally, several Koranic verse were revealed from Allah permitting the Prophet Mohammed to visit any of the women he wished. These became verses 51 and 52 in Surah 33. These verses state:

> You may put off whom you please of them, and you may take to you whom you please, and whom you desire of those whom you had separated provisionally; no blame attaches to you; this is most proper, so that their eyes may be cool and they may not grieve, and that they should be pleased, all of them, with what you give them, and Allah knows what is in your hearts; and Allah is Knowing, Forbearing.
>
> It is not allowed to you to take women afterwards, nor that you should change them for other wives, though their beauty be pleasing to you, except what your right hand possesses; and Allah is Watchful over all things

According to Imam Ghazali (1050-1111 A.D.), whose compilation of Hadith is considered authentic by Sunnis and Shias alike:

> It has been said that Hasan Ibn Ali [the Second Shia Imam and the Prophet's grandson] was a marriage addict. He married 200 wives. Sometimes he'd marry four at a time; he'd repudiate four at a time and marry new ones. Muhammad (benediction and salvation upon him) said to Hasan, 'You resemble me physically and morally.' ...It has been said that proclivity to marry often is precisely one of the similarities between Hasan and the messenger of God (benediction and salvation upon him).[21]

The evidence presented in this section clearly indicates that the Prophet did not pursue a puritanical and ascetic lifestyle.

SEXUAL PURITANISM AND ISLAM

As discussed in the previous chapter, the Koran allows a man to marry as many wives as he wishes and is allowed to have sexual access to all his female slaves or concubines. Therefore, it is clear that Islam does not prescribe an ascetic sexual lifestyle.

This alone suggests that Islamic fundamentalist puritanism has more in common with Christian puritans than with Islam, the Koran and the Prophet Mohammad.

In addition, in two passages dealing with life in Heaven, the Koran (Surah 56, Verses 16-19; and Surah 76, Verse 19) says that, in **Heaven and not on Earth**, there are eternally youthful "young boys" who will be available for sexual use by men.[22] The Arabic term used by the Koran "mokhalladoun" or in Farsi "ghalaman" refers to young boys. Apparently, for the early Muslims, homosexuality did not have the same grave moral implications it had for Jewish and Christian theologians. The Koran is essentially a covenant between an individual believer and Allah. In exchange for restraint in certain kinds of behavior on Earth, God will allow the individual to enter Heaven. Unlike some religions which believe that the soul would go to either Heaven or Hell, the Koran is very explicit that it is the person in flesh and blood who may enter Heaven or Hell.

The Koran is basically addressed to males and not to females. There are verses which are addressed to women; these verses are clear. In exchange for following the rules on Earth, in this passage, Allah promises males a Heaven in which they can have intercourse with eternally virgin girls, houris (extremely beautiful women) and eternally youthful boys. It is obvious from the verses that women are not addressed here; moreover, "youthful boys" which one suspects refers to males under the age of 14 are not sexually useful for women.[23]

In post-revolution Iran, however, homosexuals are executed. It appears that the Shariah's law condemning homosexuals to death is not based on any Koranic dictum or on the Prophet's Hadith, but rather on the Bible as well as Jewish and Christian commentaries. In the Old Testament, in Leviticus 20:13, the Bible commands that: "If a man lies with a man as one lies with a woman, both of them have done what is detestable. They must be put to death; their blood will be on their own heads."

SEXUAL PURITANISM AND HISTORICAL SHIISM

Historical Shiism is even less sexually puritanical than Sunnism. In Shia Islam, temporary marriage, *sigheh* or *mu'ta*, is allowed. Sigheh, refers to the specifically Shia practice of permitting men to have religiously sanctioned intercourse with women for a specified period of time (e.g., one hour to 99 years) in exchange for a specified amount of money.[24] For a fee, a Shia cleric arranges these sexual unions.

Unlike permanent marriage, in sigheh the permission of the father of the female is not required. It is not required that the father of the female even know about the sigheh. There is some controversy as to whether or not virgin girls can become sigheh women; the overwhelming majority of the ulama maintain they can. On the question of whether or not the father of a virgin girl should be informed and/or his permission secured for sigheh, more divergent opinions exist among the ulama; again, the overwhelming majority of the ulama maintain that neither permission nor prior knowledge on the part of the father is required. The age for females to engage in sigheh is the same as that for permanent marriage, 9-years-old, according to the Shia Shariah. It is imperative to add that for a permanent marriage, a virgin woman is required to secure the permission of the father or paternal forefather, but for a sigheh she is not.

It might seem paradoxical to require the father's permission for a 30-year-old virgin woman to get married but such permission is not required for contracting a one-hour sigheh with a virgin 9-year-old girl. This can be explained by the fact that sigheh is intended primarily for sexual enjoyment which in practice entails the union of wealthy men with indigent women. On the other hand, permanent marriage is for daughters of respectable men; in this case the patriarchal interests necessitate control of women by their fathers. In other words, ulama and other respectable members of the society may contract sigheh for themselves or for their sons but will not allow their daughters to engage in such activities which will bring shame to the family and make the daughter un-marriageable. Patriarchal and class interests include sexual access to some women and the control of others for the benefit of certain men. For all practical purposes, women who engage in sigheh are divorced or otherwise abandoned. These women do not have anyone taking care of them in a society which restricts female employment on the one hand and does not provide social security on the other.[25]

The second Shia Imam Hassan is reputed to have had somewhere between 70 to 300 wives. According to a popular belief among the Shias, "women lined up outside Imam Hassan's house to have intercourse with him; it was said that if a woman's navel touched the navel of the Imam, she would go to heaven."[26]

According to a Shia Imam "bedding a pretty wife [is] 'the best cure'; and a 'cheerful virgin's laughter and joy... alleviate all his pains.'"[27] In the words of one of the few scholars on the subject:

> Shi'i Islamic discourse celebrates marriage and sexuality as positive and self-affirming acts. Celibacy, on the other hand, is considered evil and unnatural. Islam, according to the majority of Shi'i—and Sunni—jurisconsults, is a divine religion anchored in human nature, fitrat. Its objective is to minimize human suffering and to satisfy not just the yearning of the spirit but also the burning of the flesh.[28]

CONCLUSION

Neither the Prophet Mohammad, nor Islam, nor historical Shiism is sexually puritanical. One cannot explain the ultra-puritanical mores and policies of the fundamentalists with reference to these Islamic sources. It is very hard to explain the puritanism which is reflected in the fundamentalists' punishment of males and females for simply talking and walking together and the fundamentalists' establishment of draconian segregation rules with reference to the non-puritan sexual mores of the Prophet and the Shia Imams.

Considering the plethora of conflicting sexual mores in Islam and Shiism, Islamist groups could easily find Shariah precedents for almost anything they wanted. For instance, it is very easy for a Shia group to utilize the historical practice of sigheh to promote the most lax sexual relations conceivable.[29]

Theoretically, sigheh would allow any woman or man to solicit intercourse for a fee for a specified period of time. In reality, what limits the practice is the importance of virginity in secular Iranian sexual mores. Simply put, with few exceptions, Iranian men would not marry a woman who is not virgin. This has absolutely nothing to do with either Islam or Shiism. On the other hand, a large majority of Iranians do not see any harm in talking or dancing with the opposite sex; however, the fundamentalists do. Therefore, one must make distinctions between Islam, historical Shiism, fundamentalism, and Iranian society in regards to sexual mores and relations. In other words, the puritanism of the fundamentalists is simply one variation on the sexual mores to be found in Iran. Moreover, Islamic fundamentalist sexual puritanism has more in common with 17th century Christian puritanism than with the sexual mores of either the Prophet Mohammad, Islam, historical Shiism or most Iranians.

The imposition of harsh puritanical measures by the Islamic fundamentalists has caused tremendous psychological distress in a population which regards many of these puritanical measures to be extreme. Many blame the fundamentalists' puritanism for the unusually high number of suicides among young girls and women.[30] Many journalistic reports echo observations like "...there always seems to be a shadow on the face of female pedestrians."[31] According to Mehrnaz Shahraray, a U.S.-trained female psychologist who lectures at two universities in Iran and does clinical work at home, "I don't like the way I dress [and] there is this psychological conflict.... I am wearing something I don't believe in. There is cognitive dissonance."[32] In the words of an unnamed female Iranian university professor, "There is a tremendous amount of depression, complex problems that we cannot resolve. We are depressed, we are fighting, but we are not getting very far.... I don't know how long it will take but we just can't maintain the status quo."[33]

Many women find it very humiliating and insulting to be told by total strangers (various members of the para-military moral patrols) that their dress or behavior is unacceptable. Women (and to a lesser extent men also) have to develop two personalities, one public, another, an authentic one at home.[34] It is not the sexual mores of Islam, the Koran, the Prophet Mohammad or historical Shiism that is to blame for the extreme puritanism of the fundamentalists. On this particular issue (sexual mores) it appears that Islam is not even a contributing factor. The sexual puritanism that is found among Shia fundamentalists in Iran and among the Sunni fundamentalists elsewhere has more in common with the sexual puritanism of Christian puritans than with any Islamic ones.

CHAPTER 6

CONCLUSION

I n this book, I have analyzed the relationship between Islam and the misogynist policies of Khomeini and his fundamentalist followers. Based on this study we can make the following conclusions. First, the fact that anti-feminist ideologies and policies are advocated by non-Islamic groups as well as Islamic ones indicates that Islam is not the necessary factor for anti-feminism.

Second, the fact that some Islamic groups such as the liberal Islamists (i.e., LMI), communist Islamists (i.e., PMOI) are both Islamic and believe in the equality between the sexes, as well as secular groups, who are personally devout (i.e., INF) who advocate gender equality indicates that Islam is not the sufficient factor for anti-feminism.

Third, the fact that the Koran contains verses which are clearly patriarchal and discriminatory against women allows anti-feminist groups, such as the fundamentalists, to use these verses to undermine the positions of those who advocate gender equality. However, Islamic fundamentalists also advocate sexual puritanism which is alien to the mores of the Prophet Mohammad, the Koran, early Islam, and historical Shiism. Therefore, Islam may be a contributing factor for policies which discriminates against women.

Islamic fundamentalists, like other Islamic groups, pick and choose from the rich, variegated and contraaictory values in Islam whatever suits their interests. This of course is nothing new. In the past 1400 years, Islam has been used to provide justifications for slavery, pre-capitalist mercantile economy, landed property (e.g., landlord/sharecropper relations), capitalism, socialism, communism, feminism and anti-feminism.

If the analysis in this book is correct, Islam should be understood as the medium through which anti-feminism is expressed (e.g., Islamic fundamentalism). In other words, Islam provides "justifications" for anti-feminism which anti-feminist groups can draw upon in their struggle against gender equality. In this context then, Islam may be understood as a contributing factor in the success of anti-feminist policies and legislations.

ARE JUDAISM AND CHRISTIANITY ANY DIFFERENT?

There is no question that women in Islamic countries are more oppressed than their counterparts in Europe, and the United States (and in much of the world). Could this disparity be explained by the difference between Islam on the one hand and Judaism and Christianity on the other. In this section I demonstrate that Judaism and Christianity share many anti-feminist values with Islam. If my analysis is right, the political ramification of my argument is that changing one's religion form Islam to Judaism or Christianity will not help the struggle for gender egalitarianism.[1]

Judaism and Christianity are equally as anti-feminist as Islam. For example, according to the Old Testament, woman is clearly created to serve man. After God had created the Garden of Eden and Adam, according to Genesis 2:18, "The Lord God said: It is not good for the man to be alone, I will make a **helper** suitable for him." (my emphasis).

After the livestock, birds and beasts were introduced to Adam for naming them, the Bible goes on to say in Genesis 2:20-22,

> So the man gave names to all the livestock, the birds of the air and all the beasts of the field. But for Adam no **suitable helper** was found. So the Lord God caused the man to fall into a deep sleep; and while he was sleeping, he took one of the man's ribs and closed up the place with flesh. Then the Lord God made a woman from the rib he had taken out of the man, and he brought her to the man.

It appears that God decided to create Eve because none of the animals was found to be a suitable helper for Adam. In other words, women, like animals, were created for the purpose of serving man.

As if the reason for the creation of woman was not clear enough to justify patriarchal domination, those who wrote the Old Testament felt that a more direct justification was necessary. Therefore, the Old Testament goes on to say that after the woman ate the fruit of "the tree of the knowledge of good and evil," God told the woman: "I will greatly increase your pains in childbearing: with pain you will give birth to children, Your desire will be for your husband, and **he will rule over you**." (Genesis 3:16) (emphasis mine).

The writers of the New Testament were even more clear than those who wrote the Old Testament. In Ephesians 5:22-24, the New Testament writes:

> Wives, submit to your husbands as to the Lord. For the husband is the head of the wife as Christ is the head of the church, his body, of which he is the Savior. Now as the church submits to Christ, so also wives should submit to their husbands in everything.

The same theme is repeated in 1 Peter 3:1-2 in the New Testament:

> Wives, in the same way be submissive to your husbands so that, if any of them do not believe the word, they may be won over without words by the behavior of their wives, when they see the purity and reverence of your lives.

The Bible states that women are created to serve men and must submit to their husbands, and men are the rulers of women. Unlike in the Judeo-Christian myth of creation, in the Islamic myth, Adam and Eve were both created simultaneously from the same soil.[2] This allows feminists in polities with Muslim population to quote the relevant verse to support their position. Anti-feminists in the Judeo-Christian tradition could easily quote the Bible to buttress their position.

Moreover, in Islamic history there are several females who were extremely powerful politically, economically and religiously. Khadijeh, the Prophet's first wife who was one of the wealthiest merchants in Mecca was the first person to become Muslim. Ayesha, the Prophet's influential wife personally raised and led an army against Imam Ali's rule (in the War of Camel).[3]

An Islamic motto says: "Take half of your religion from Ayesha."[4] Fatimah, the Prophet's favorite daughter was also active in politics and publicly campaigned on behalf of Imam Ali's (her husband) and her own right to inherit a piece of expensive orchard which had been given in trust to her father. Zahra, the Prophet's granddaughter, and the daughter of Ali and Fatimah, also took a public role and defended the right of her brother Hussein to become caliph.

In the Judeo-Christian tradition the patriarchal ideology is less inconsistent, while Islamic scriptures, mythologies and histories offer role models for women which allow for greater power and less inequality. Although women and men are not equal in Islam, there are Koranic verses and Hadiths that may allow Islamists who are feminist to draw upon in their struggles against gender inequality.

Islam, Judaism and Christianity contain core beliefs which are categorically unscientific. All three Abrahamic religions today have fundamentalist and non-fundamentalist interpretations and sects.[5] For example, fundamentalist Christians literally believe that Noah lived 950 years because the Old Testament in Genesis 9:28-29 states: "After the flood Noah lived 350 years. Altogether, Noah lived 950 years, and then he died." Moreover, fundamentalist Christians oppose the overwhelming scientific evidence for evolution because the Bible states that the creation occurred in seven days in Genesis 1:1-31 and 2:1-4. Likewise, fundamentalist Jews reject the scientific evidence for the existence and extinction of dinosaurs, because as Rabbi Moshe Gafner (who speaks for the Agudat Israel Rabbinical court which pronounces kosher endorsements, among other things), says: "The dinosaur represents a heresy against the creation of the world by the Blessed Creator," and the notion that dinosaurs lived millions of years ago contradicts explicit religious teaching that the Earth is less than 6,000 years old.[6] Despite explicit anti-scientific teachings of Christianity and Judaism, polities which adhere to them have witnessed scientific progress.

A common logical fallacy is to denote causal significance to the scripture when there is a correspondence between the actions of the religious followers and a particular verse. In other words, when one observes a practice among the followers of a religion the wrong deduction could be reached that that practice is caused by the religion. However, we can observe that believers do things that contradict their scriptures. For example, the respective scriptures in Judaism, Christianity and Islam affirm slavery as a normal, moral and ethical practice.

According to the Bible, slavery is justified as the punishment of a sin which was committed by Noah's son Ham, (the father of Canaan). As the result of Ham's sin, all of his descendant beginning with Canaan were to become slaves of other people who were descendant of Noah's other two sons. Although no race is directly identified with Canaan in the Bible or in the Koran, all Jewish, Christian and Islamic commentaries have identified Canaan to have been born black (as coal) and inhabiting Africa.[7] According to the Old Testament, Genesis 9:18-27,

> The sons of Noah who came out of the ark were Shem, Ham and Japheth. (Ham was the father of Canaan.) These were the three sons of Noah, and from them came the people who were scattered over the earth.
>
> Noah, a man of the soil, proceeded to plant a vineyard. When he drank some of its wine, he became drunk and lay uncovered inside his tent. Ham, the father of Canaan, saw his father's nakedness and told his two brothers outside. But Shem and Japheth took a garment and laid it across their shoulders; then they walked in backward and covered their father's nakedness. Their faces were turned the other way so that they would not see their father's nakedness.
>
> When Noah awoke from his wine and found out what his youngest son had done to him he said, "Cursed be Canaan! The lowest of slaves will he be to his brothers."
>
> He also said, "Blessed be the Lord, the God of Shem! May Canaan be the slave of Shem. May God extend the territory of Japheth; may Japheth live in the tents of Shem, and may Canaan be his (or their) slave."

The New Testament does not merely accepts slavery, but it vigorously promotes and justifies it. In other words, slavery is not accepted as a necessary evil but is promoted as a divine institution. Slaves are told to obey their slave-masters as a religious duty. In Ephesians 6:5-8, the New Testaments writes:

> Slaves, obey your earthly masters with respect and fear, and with sincerity of heart, just as you would obey Christ. Obey them not only to win their favor when their eye is on you, but like slaves of Christ, doing the will of God from your heart. Serve wholeheartedly, as if you were serving the Lord, not men, because you know that the Lord will reward everyone for whatever good he does, whether he is slave or free.

The same theme is emphasized in 1 Timothy 6:1-2 in the New Testament:

> All who are under the yoke of slavery should consider their masters worthy of full respect, so that God's name and our teaching may not be

slandered. Those who have believing masters are not to show less respect for them because they are brothers. Instead, they are to serve them even better, because those who benefit from their service are believers, and dear to them. These are the things you are to teach and urge on them.

The same theme is repeated in 1 Peter 2:18-21 in the New Testament:

Slaves, submit yourselves to your masters with all respect, not only to those who are good and considerate, but also to those who are harsh. For it is commendable if a man bears up under the pain of unjust suffering because he is conscious of God. But how is it to your credit if you receive a beating for doing wrong and endure it? But if you suffer for doing good and you endure it, this is commendable before God. To this you were called, because Christ suffered for you, leaving you an example, that you should follow in his steps.

If Jews, Christians, and Muslims were to practice everything in their holy scriptures they should all allow and practice slavery. Today the overwhelming majority of practicing Jews, Christians and Muslims regard slavery as immoral, not because of what their respective scripture say, but despite them. In other words, in one moment in history slave societies drew upon the respective scriptures to justify slavery, today when slavery is out of practice, they simply ignore those scriptural principles.

Another relevant example might be the explicit injunction in the Old Testament that all homosexual men should be put to death. In Leviticus 20:13, the Old Testament states:

If a man lies with a man as one lies with a woman, both of them have done what is detestable. They must be put to death; their blood will be on their own heads.

With the exception of the KKK, I know of no major Christian or Jewish group which calls for the implementation of this Biblical injunction. Clearly to implement this Biblical injunction, male homosexuals who account for between two and four percent of each human population "must be put to death." In the United States, with a population of 260 million, it would come to somewhere between 5.2 and 10.4 million men.

And if one intends to implement every word of the Old Testament, he "must put to death" anyone who "curses his father and mother," (Leviticus 20:9), anyone who "commits adultery" (Leviticus 20:10), any man who "has sexual relations with an animal" (Leviticus 20:15), any woman who "approaches an animal to have sexual relations" with (Leviticus 20:16). In addition, the hapless animals in the last two instances must be put to death as well (Leviticus 20:15-16).

Considering the fact that the core religious beliefs of the three Abrahamic religions are remarkably close, assigning dissimilar sets of behaviors, values, and politics to each is a mistake. The fact that European and American women have more rights and freedoms than their Muslim counterparts cannot be explained by reference to the holy texts in Christianity and Islam. In other words, it is not Christianity which has given women rights. On the contrary it has been the struggles of courageous feminists (men and women) in Western countries who have struggled against gender inequality. Women in Western polities and Israel have more rights than their counterparts in Islamic countries not because of Christianity and Judaism, but despite them.

POLICY IMPLICATIONS FOR THOSE STRUGGLING FOR GENDER EQUALITY

If the analysis in this book is right, to achieve a more gender equal society, women in Muslim countries should struggle for a secular polity. It is clear that the more a society is secular, the higher is the likelihood that men and women are equal in that polity. And the weaker religious fundamentalists (of any religion) are, the likelihood that men and women are equal increases in that polity. Because the relationship between religion and gender inequality have been shown to be a contributing factor we should pay close attention to the historical, political and cultural contexts of each society. However, *ceteris paribus*, if one wants to see more equality between men and women, one should struggle for a secular polity in general and struggle against religious fundamentalists in particular.

The secular project, or the relationship between religion and politics is not merely of academic interest to the people of the Middle East. For the past 200 years, Westerners have been able to dominate the Middle East politically, militarily, economically, technologically and culturally. Western domination has been traumatic and deeply humiliating to the people of the Middle East.

If the people of the Middle East are to catch up with the West, I believe that the best way, and perhaps the only way, is simply to do what the

Europeans did: to start a new enlightenment. In other words, to begin the process of separating both mosque and state, as well as religion and politics. This process may begin by respecting freedom of expression in political, scientific and cultural issues together with complete freedom of political parties and the press.

It appears to me that this process of enlightenment is a necessary condition for progress. It is not the only ingredient, but without it the people of the Middle East will continue to be mired in their centuries-long backwardness, inequality and despotism. Needless to say, it is the ruling classes and clerics besides the foreign powers, who benefit from such a state of underdevelopment.

The Christian Inquisition led to the Enlightenment in Europe. Perhaps one of the reactions to Islamic fundamentalism might be a movement by Middle Eastern intellectuals and masses to start a new enlightenment. If that actually does occur, it will be the most redeeming contribution of Islamic fundamentalism.

APPENDIX 1
IDEOLOGIES OF POLITICAL PARTIES AND POLITICIANS IN IRAN 1979-1984

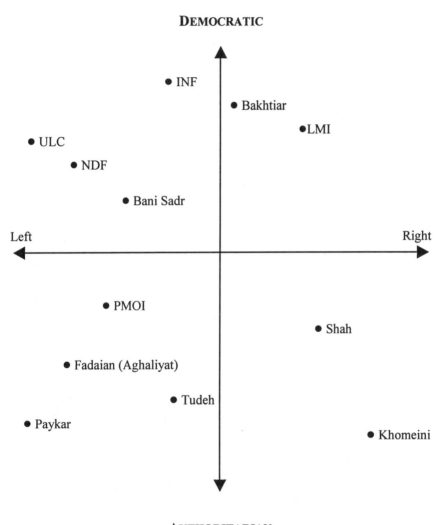

DEMOCRATIC

- INF
- Bakhtiar
- LMI
- ULC
- NDF
- Bani Sadr

Left   Right

- PMOI
- Shah
- Fadaian (Aghaliyat)
- Tudeh
- Paykar
- Khomeini

AUTHORITARIAN

See Glossary. The X-axis reflects proposed/actual economic policies/demands. The Y-axis reflects proposed/actual political structures; those advocating free multiparty elections and civil liberties are classified as "DEMOCRATIC," and those advocating single-party system and denying civil liberties to opponents are classified as "AUTHORITARIAN."

APPENDIX 2
IDEOLOGIES OF POLITICAL PARTIES
AND POLITICIANS IN IRAN 2001.

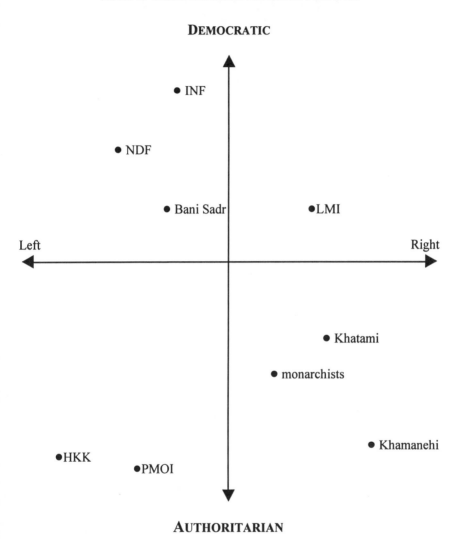

DEMOCRATIC

• INF

• NDF

• Bani Sadr   •LMI

Left   Right

• Khatami

• monarchists

• Khamanehi

•HKK

•PMOI

AUTHORITARIAN

See Glossary. The X-axis reflects proposed/actual economic policies/demands. The Y-axis reflects proposed/actual political structures; those advocating free multiparty elections and civil liberties are classified as "DEMOCRATIC," and those advocating single-party system and denying civil liberties to opponents are classified as "AUTHORITARIAN."

NOTES TO CHAPTER 1

1. I owe the following examples to Glossop, *Confronting War: An Examination of Humanity's Most Pressing Problem*, pp. 40-41.
2. On July 29, 1991, for instance, in Isfahan (a large city which is considered to be among the most traditional cities in Iran) when the newly formed Niroyeh Entezami tried to arrest several women, whose veil was not covering every strand of their hair, the people intervened. A riot ensued in which over 300 people were arrested; see *Iran Times*, August 2, 1991, p. 16 and *Iran Times*, August 16, 1991, pp. 1, 12.
3. Afsaneh Najmabadi, "Hazards of Modernity and Morality: Women, State and Ideology in Contemporary Iran," in *Women, Islam and the State*, ed. Deniz Kandiyoti, pp. 63f. According to El Saadawi, the dominant view on the oppression and the inferior position of Arab women also gives causal significance to Islam; see Nawal El Saadawi, "Women and Islam," in *Women's Studies International Forum*, vol. 5, no. 2, (1982), p. 202.
4. For example refer to Azar Tabari, "Islam and the Struggle for Emancipation of Iranian Women," and Haleh Afshar, "Khomeini's Teachings and Their Implications for Iranian Women," both in *In the Shadow of Islam: The Women's Movement in Iran*, eds. Tabari and Yeganeh; Farah Azari, ed. *Women of Iran: The Conflict with Fundamentalist Islam*.
5. Eliz Sanasarian, *The Woman's Rights Movement in Iran*, pp. 133-134.
6. Afshar, "Women, State and Ideology in Iran," in *Third World Quarterly*, vol. 17, no. 2, April 1985.
7. Mahdavi, "The Position of Women in Shi'a Iran: Views of the 'Ulama," in *Women and the Family in the Middle East: New Voices of Change*, ed., Elizabeth Fernea, pp. 255, 265-6.
8. For an extensive discussion of the various paradigms in the study of Islamic fundamentalism refer to Masoud Kazemzadeh, "Teaching the Politics of Islamic Fundamentalism," in *PS: Political Science and Politics*, vol. 31, no. 1 (March 1998).

9. Parvin Paidar, *Women and the Political Process in Twentieth-Century Iran*, p. 232.
10. See my review of her book in *American Political Science Review*, vol. 90, no. 4 (December 1996), pp. 929-931.
11. Najmabadi, "Hazards of Modernity," pp. 63f.
12. Valentine M. Moghadam, *Modernizing Women: Gender and Social Change in the Middle East*, p. 5. I would like to thank Valentine Moghadam for referring me back to this quote.
13. Ibid., p. 6.

NOTES TO CHAPTER 2

1. A Western reporter estimated the demonstrators to be in the tens of thousands; see Ray Vicker, "Women in Iran Take To Streets in a Move To Preserve Rights: Many Fear an Islamic State, Balk at Traditional Dress; Effect on the Ayatollah," in *The Wall Street Journal*, March 12, 1979, p. 1. More than 18 years of the fundamentalist rule has not reduced the saliency of the issue of hejab. In the words of a *New York Times* reporter, "...the most heated battle for women's rights is still fought through their wardrobes." See Elaine Sciolino, "The Will to Adorn, the Will of Allah," in *New York Times*, May 24, 1992.
2. Jane O'Reilly, "The Unfinished Revolution: For Iran's Women, the real Struggle Goes on," in *Time Magazine*, April 2, 1979.
3. For a compilation of the slogans of the March 8, 1979, march refer to *Nimeye Digar: Persian Language Feminist Journal*, no. 10, Winter 1990, p. 196.
4. For a comprehensive account of this important episode see Azar Tabari and Nahid Yeganeh, eds. *In the Shadow of Islam: The Women's Movement in Iran*; and Eliz Sanasarian, *The Women's Rights Movement in Iran*.
5. Cheryl Benard, "Islam and Women: Some Reflections on the Experience of Iran," in *Journal of South Asian and Middle Eastern Studies*, vol. IV, no., 2, Winter 1980, p. 13. According to this source the number of women marchers is estimated at 15,000; Benard further adds that the women "occupied the Palace of Justice for three hours."
6. See PMOI's proclamation issued on March 12, 1979 republished in *In the Shadow of Islam: The Women's Movement in Iran*, eds., Tabari and Yeganeh, pp. 126-127.
7. The term "misogynist" is used to mean a set of policies and actions which take away women's existing rights by coercion. When policies, actions or ideas deny the equality of the sexes and no coercion is implied, I use the term "anti-feminist."

8. It is imperative to mention that the only major organization which came to the defense of female judges was the Iran National Front. All other political organizations including the incumbent liberal Islamists, communist Islamist PMOI, and the secular communists remained silent. See the proclamation of INF's Women's Organization in calling for a public rally to oppose Khomeini's dismissal order in *In the Shadow of Islam: the Women's Movement in Iran*, Tabari and Yeganeh, pp. 227-228.

9. For the December 1979 conference and the reaction of the leftist forces towards them refer to Eliz Sanasarian, "An Analysis of Fida'i and Mujahidin Positions on Women's Rights." For July 5 demonstrations refer to Nesta Ramazani, "Behind the Veil: Status of Women in Revolutionary Iran," in *Journal of South Asian and Middle Eastern Studies*, vol. IV, no. 2, Winter 1980, p. 27.

10. Cited in Janet Bauer, "Iranian Women: How many Faces Behind the Veil?" in *East-West Perspectives: Journal of the East-West Center*, vol. 1, no. 4, Fall 1980, p. 21.

11. *Iran Times*, September 4, 1992, pp. 1, 12.

12. See *The Old Testament*, 2 Chronicles 36:20-23 and Ezra 1:1-8. For an excellent commentary on the influence of Persians and Zoroastrians on the development of Jewish theology and the incorporation of Zoroastrian beliefs into Jewish theological concepts see Bernard Lewis, *The Middle East: A Brief History of the Last 2,000 Years*, pp. 27-28.

13. Don Peretz, *The Middle East Today*, 5th ed., p. 39.

14. Interview with Dr. Jalil SazgarNejad in *Roznameh Iran*, Tir 25 and 26, 1380 (Iranian calendar) published in Iran, and placed on the internet: <www.iran-emrooz.de/goftgu/sazgan800429.html>

15. Middle East Watch, *Guardians of Thought: Limits on Freedom of Expression in Iran*, p. 123.

16. Habib Ladjevardi, *Labor Unions and Autocracy in Iran*.

17. Habib Ladjevardi, "The Origins of U.S. Support for an Autocratic Iran," in *IJMES*, vol. 15, no. 2, May 1983; *idem, Labour Unions and Autocracy in Iran*; Mark Gasiorowski, "The 1953 Coup d'Etat in Iran," in *IJMES*, vol. 19, no. 3, August 1987.

18. See Eliz Sanasarian, *The Women's Rights Movement in Iran*, ch. 7, esp. pp. 147-148; Farah Azari, "The Post-Revolutionary Women's Movement in Iran," in *Women of Iran: The Conflict with Fundamentalist Islam*; Nahid Yeganeh, "Women's Struggles in the Islamic Republic of Iran," in *In the Shadow of Islam: The Women's Movement in Iran*, eds. Tabari and Yeganeh; Az, "The Women's Struggle in Iran," in *Monthly Review*, vol. 32, no. 10, March 1981.

19. Ray Vicker, "Women in Iran Take To Streets in a Move To Preserve Rights: Many Fear an Islamic State, Balk at Traditional Dress; Effect on the Ayatollah," in *The Wall Street Journal*, March 12, 1979, pp. 1, 24; Jane O'Reilly, "The Unfinished Revolution: For Iran's Women, the Real Struggle Goes On," in *Time Magazine*, April 2, 1979, pp. 34, 37.

20. Constance Elizabeth Maud, "The First Persian Feminist," in *The Fortnightly Review*, vol. 93, January to June 1913, pp. 1175-82, esp. p. 1180.

21. Mary Winsor, "The Blossoming of a Persian Feminist," in *Equal Rights*, the publication of National Women's Party, October 23, 1926, pp. 293-294. According to Winsor, the feminist journal that Ms. Dolatabadi published had a circulation of 2500.

22. Annie Woodman Stocking, "The New Woman In Persia," in *The Muslim World*, vol. 2, no. 4, October 1912, p. 367.

23. As told by a progressive young Iranian woman feminist to Ms. Stocking. See Stocking, ibid., pp. 371-372.

24. Shuster, *The Strangling of Persia*, p. 198.

25. Janet Afary, "On the Origins of Feminism in Early 20th-Century Iran," in *Journal of Women's History*, vol. 1, no. 2, Fall 1989, p. 78.

26. William Morgan Shuster, *The Strangling of Persia*, pp. 191f.

27. Shuster, p. 193.

28. No author, "The New Woman In Persia," in *The Muslim World*, vol. 1, no. 2, April 1911, p. 186. In Iran, first cousins are permitted to marry, and historically it had been the most preferred match. The custom of marriage between first cousins is still common in small towns and villages and among the traditional sectors.

29. The fatva was issued in 1948; see Edward Mortimer, *Faith and Power*, p. 311.

30. Under intense pressure from Kashani and Brujerdi (the two highest ranked ulama at the time), who declared that it was contrary to Islamic law, Mossadegh withdrew the bill franchising women; see Henry Munson, Jr., *Islam and Revolution in the Middle East*, p. 51. Munson adds, "One person was killed and ten seriously wounded when religious students in Qom staged a demonstration to protest the idea of extending voting rights to women."

31. Mortimer, *Faith and Power*, pp. 314f. He further adds, "But the first issue to bring direct conflict was the government's land reform Bill.... Thanks to religious endowments built up since Safavid times, the *ulama* owned or controlled large areas of land..." Ayatollah Bihbihani (also spelled Behbahani) was the third highest cleric after Brujerdi and Kashani; all three of whom supported the Shah in the CIA-organized coup in August 1953. Ayatollah Behbahani was particularly effective in mobilizing the lumpenproletariat of South Tehran with CIA money.

32. Najmabadi, "Hazards of Modernity and Morality," p. 63.

33. Moreover the Constitution specifically excludes women from the top four positions in the government. It directly and *de jure* excludes women from the position of president and prime minister. And indirectly it excludes women from both the Supreme Leader (the highest position in the Islamic Republic) and the head of the Council of Guardians by requiring the respective occupants to be a *marjah taghlid*--a high ranking cleric.
34. *Iran Times*, July 19, 1991, p. 5.
35. Marilyn Frye, *The Politics of Reality: Essays in Feminist Theory*.
36. "The Constitution of the Islamic Republic of Iran," Articles 5, 107, 109 require the Supreme Leader to be a mojtahed. According to Khomeini one should follow a mojtahed who is "a male, mature, sane, 12-Imami Shia, not-illegitimate, alive and just." See Khomeini, *Tozih al-Masael*, (Clarification of Questions), p. 1, Problem 2. These are of course the basic prerequisites for becoming a mojtahed; for further qualification see Problems 3-14 in ibid.
37. Preamble to the Constitution, p. 3. The words in the parentheses are in the original.
38. For a feminist critique of the Constitution refer to Sanasarian, *The Women's Rights Movement in Iran*, pp. 131-3.
39. Tabari and Yeganeh, eds. *In the Shadow of Islam*, p. 94."Article 91: Adultery is proved on the basis of testimonies by four righteous men, or three righteous men and two righteous women....""Article 92: In cases where adultery would lead to flogging it could also be proved on the basis of the testimonies by two righteous men or four righteous women." "Note: Women's testimonies alone or accompanied by one righteous man's testimony do not prove adultery, but those witnesses will receive punishment for libel."Ibid., p. 95.
40. "Article 5: If a Muslim man willfully murders a Muslim woman, he will be sentenced to death but the woman's guardian must pay the murderer one half of a man's blood-money before he receives the death penalty." [blood-money is determined on the basis of one's wealth, so the blood-money for a rich man is more than what it is for a poor man.] "Article 6: If a Muslim woman willfully murders a Muslim man she will be sentenced only to death and will not have to pay anything to the guardians of the blood." ["Guardians of the blood" refers to inheritors of the person except husband or wife.] "Article 46: If a man murders a woman, the guardian of the blood has the choice of carrying out the death **and** paying the murderer one half of the full amount of the blood-money, **or** demanding the woman's blood-money from the murderer." The words in brackets and emphases are mine. Compiled in Tabari and Yeganeh, *In the Shadow of Islam*, p. 94.
41. For an analysis of the Civil Code prior to the revolution refer to Gholam-Reza Vatandoust, "The Status of Iranian Women During the Pahlavi Regime," in *Women and the Family in Iran*, ed. Asghar Fathi.

42. Revised Law #1043 of Civil Code : "Permission of marriage for a female who has never been married, even though she has reached the adult age, is vested in her father or paternal fore-father (i.e., grand-father, great grand-father). If father or paternal fore-father without stating legitimate reason does not grant his permission, the female can ask the proper civil court (after introducing the man and the conditions of marriage and dowry between the couple), which will inform the father or paternal fore-father; and after 15 days from the receipt of information and lack of response from the 'said guardian' the said court can grant the permission for marriage." Revised Law #1044 of Civil Code : "If father or paternal fore-father is not in the area...the girl can request the court's permission, after submitting the required information...." Both cited in *Iran Times*, September 6, 1991, p. 12 (my translation).

43. See Mehrdad Darwishpoor, "Divorce Among Immigrant Iranians," in *Iran Times*, June 17, 1994, p. 9, (in Farsi).

44. Youssef Ibrahim, "Some in Iran Finding Islamic Law Harsh, Its Justice Swift," in *The New York Times*, March 1, 1979.

45. For a comprehensive treatment of the Family Protection Act (or Law) refer to Vatandoust, "The Status of Iranian Women," op. cit., see p. 115 for the point just made in the text.

46. For Hojatolislam Morteza Moghtadaee's comments see *Iran Times*, February 28, 1992, p. 5. Mr. Moghtadaee was the Chief of the Supreme Court of the Islamic Republic.

47. These circumstances include: (1) the husband has disappeared for more than 3 years; (2) the husband is sexually impotent, which requires a two-year waiting period and a physician's certification, (3) the husband is infertile as documented by physician's certification; (4) the husband has become insane; (4) the husband has become physically disabled; and lastly, (5) the marriage agreement stipulated that the husband has granted his divorce rights to his wife. The last condition was extremely rare because in Iranian culture to talk about divorce prior to marriage is a bad omen.

48. Mehrdad Darwishpoor, in *Iran Times*, June 24, 1994, p. 11. In the years 1955, 1960, and 1965, the number of divorces per 1000 persons was 1.3, 1.2, and 1, respectively (this statistic should not to be confused with the rate of divorce per marriage).

49. Vatandoust, "The Status of Iranian Women," p. 121.

50. All data and analyses are based on Mehrdad Darwishpoor, op. cit.

51. Ibid.

52. Vatandoust, "The Status of Iranian Women," p. 121.

53. See Vatandoust, "The Status of Iranian Women," Table 2, p. 122.

54. Ibid. For the 1986 numbers, there might be other contributing factors besides the new laws promulgated by the fundamentalists such as the economic crisis, the war with Iraq, and the resentment of educated modern middle class

women towards patriarchal pressures which fundamentalists policies entailed.

55. According to Shireen Mahdavi, "Shawhar Ahu Khanum: Passion, Polygyny and Tragedy," in *Middle Eastern Studies*, vol. 24, no. 1, January 1988, the justifications for polygyny are "shortage of men, orphans and women's need for sex," and that "it is better to formalize the male's polygamous desires than to force him to have extra-marital sex as in other societies."

56. Oriana Fallaci, "An Interview With Khomeini," in *New York Times Magazine*, October 7, 1979, p. 31. I was referred back to this quote by Sanasarian, *The Women's Rights Movement in Iran*, p. 134.

57. Islamic Republic of Iran, Plan and Budget Organization, Statistical Centre of Iran, *Iran Statistical Yearbook 1369 [March 1990-March 1991]*, Table 2-2, p. 33.

58. Ibid.

59. Cited in *Iran Times*, December 4, 1992, p. 11. Until the Revolution, the number of polygynous marriages was in decline.

60. Shireen Mahdavi, "The Position of Women in Shi'a Iran: Views of the 'Ulama," in *Women and the Family in the Middle East*, ed. Elizabeth Fernea.

61. In both Latin America and the Middle East the typical middle class boy's first sexual experience is usually with a maid who works in his or a neighbor's house or with a prostitute. There are many such similarities in the Third World--in both Islamic and non-Islamic polities.

62. Reynaldo Galindo Pohl, "Report of the Special Representative of the U.N. Commission of Human Rights on Iran," in *Iran Times*, February 25, 1994, p. 11.

63. Cited in Mehrdad Darwishpoor.

64. *Iran Times*, January 8, 1993, p. 12.

65. Ibid.

66. The Shia Shariah specifically forbids three occupations for women: judgeship, issuing a fatva (i.e., becoming a high-ranking cleric), and political leadership. There is a controversy on jihad; some argue that the Shariah only requires men to engage in jihad (i.e., women are not required but could participate), others maintain that women are forbidden. It is noteworthy to point out that in September 1994, the Ministry of Justice submitted a bill to the Majles which asked that women be allowed to become judges. The Director of the Personnel of the Ministry of Justice announced that in 1994 there were 140 women with law degrees who served as contract employees (as opposed to permanent employees) who could become both permanent and judges if the bill passes. Moreover, he added that annually about 400 male graduates of law schools were employed by the ministry. See *Iran Times*, October 7, 1994, p. 5.

67. Rahnema and Nomani, op. cit., p. 220.

68. Interview with Ms. Saaideh, Esq.; St. Louis, March 1991.

69. "On the Situation of Iranian Women: A Report From Iran," in *Payam Azadi*, op. cit., (organ of the United Left Council). Haleh Afshar, "Women, State and Ideology in Iran" in *Third World Quarterly*, vol. 17, no. 2, April 1985. Farah Azari, "The Post-Revolutionary Women's Movement in Iran," *Women of Iran: The Conflict with Fundamentalist Islam*, p. 193. Azar Tabari, "Chronology" in *Nimeye Digar: Persian Language Feminist Quarterly*, vol. 1, no. 2, Autumn 1984, pp. 127-134. Interview with Ms. Saaideh, Esq., St. Louis, March 1991. In her research, Valentine Moghadam has found that an extremely small number of women have been allowed to enter law schools. Personal correspondence, September 13, 1991.

70. *Iran Times*, April 15, 1994, p. 5.

71. *Zanan* (Women), a semi-governmental women's magazine established in Bahman 1370 (January-February 1992) with the explicit aim of attracting educated women back to work cited the figure of 440,000 as the approximate number of women who lost employment in the **private sector alone** in the period under consideration. See *Zanan*, no. 1, Bahman 1370.

72. These calculations are mine based on the 1976 and 1986 census data. See Islamic Republic of Iran, Plan and Budget Organization, Statistical Centre of Iran, *Iran Statistical Yearbook 1369*, Table 2-1, p. 33.

73. *Iran Times*, December 11, 1992, p. 11, and *Iran Times*, December 10, 1993.

74. Moghadam, *Modernizing Women*, p. 177; Sanasarian, *The Women's Rights Movement in Iran*, pp. 136-7.

75. See Moghadam, "Women, Work, and Ideology in the Islamic Republic," in *IJMES*, vol. 20, no. 2 May 1988, p. 242, note 34.

76. A 2.6% decrease from the 8.5% is a 31% reduction.

77. A decrease of 3% from 60.7% is a relative decrease of 5%.

78. *Iran Times*, December 10, 1993.

79. Many women with higher education were teachers, nurses and physicians whose jobs were more secure from fundamentalist purge drives than those of women who were employed in factories and offices. In Iran the overwhelming number of white-collar employees, both male and female, either possess a high school diploma or less.

80. See Val Moghadam, *Modernizing Women: Gender and Social Change in the Middle East*, pp. 40, 47, Tables 2.2 and 2.5.

81. Moghadam attributed the increase in unemployment among female blue collar workers to the "fact that most of these women were employed in the multinational corporations (MNCs). When the latter closed down or changed owners, preferential treatment in hiring practices was accorded to men." See Moghadam, "Women, Work, and Ideology in The Islamic Republic," in *IJMES*, vol. 20, no. 2, May 1988, p. 233.

82. Reported in *Iran Times*, December 18, 1992, p. 11.

83. Ibid.

84. Ibid.
85. US Government, Department of the Army, *Iran: A Country Study- Area Handbook Series 1989*, p. 132.
86. Ibid.
87. Abrahamian, *Iran Between Two Revolutions*, p. 434. For a detailed breakdown and analyses of the massive increase of education for women see Jacquiline R. Touba, "Sex Segregation and Women's Roles in the Economic System: The Case of Iran," in *Research in the Interweave of Social Roles: Women and Men*, ed. Helena Z. Lopata, pp. 51-98, esp. p. 86.
88. The secular liberal democratic Iran National Front which most of the university faculty and administrators constituted its supporters strongly opposed Khomeini's attack on the universities. Two communist organizations popular among university students Fadaian-Minority Faction and Paykar took up arms and defended their headquarters at Tehran University. The newly-elected Bani Sadr (liberal Islamist) gave his verbal support after the fact that Khomeini and fundamentalists had started attacking universities. The communist-Islamist PMOI evacuated its headquarters at Tehran University and called up others to evacuate the campus. The pro-Moscow conventional communist party, Tudeh Party, evacuated its headquarters at Tehran University as well.
89. Sahar Ghahreman, "The Islamic Government Policy Towards Women's Access to Higher Education in Iran," in *Nimeye Digar: Persian Language Feminist Journal*, no. 7, Summer 1988, p. 24 (in Farsi). The first provision was intended to exclude atheists, in particular secular liberals, socialists and Marxists. The second provision was intended to exclude the Islamic and Islamist opponents of fundamentalists in particular.
90. In one case, a female student who had received the highest score in Konkor in the province of Bakhtaran was denied entrance because she was considered not Islamic enough. The reason that she was barred from the medical school was that after the interview she shook the hand of the chief interviewer who had extended his hand to congratulate her for passing the interview. In another case a female from Tabriz was not allowed to enter medical school because upon further investigation by the political-ideological commissars, it was found that she was not a fundamentalist. In the latter case, several members of the political-ideological commissars posing as non-fundamentalist parents of a prospective husband went to the small grocery store on the corner of the alley next to her house and asked the grocery store owner--who had known the family for over twenty year--about her. After asking several questions about her modesty and character, in a nonchalant manner they asked for reassurance that she was not a fundamentalist. The grocery store owner reassured the group that she was not incompatible with the prospective family. In both cases the female students went to Turkey and

succeeded in entering medical school there. Both are currently specialists: one is a radiologist, another is an ophthalmologist. Personal interviews.

91. Ghahreman, op. cit., p. 25.
92. Ibid.
93. Ibid., pp. 24-25.
94. *Iran Times*, July 17, 1992, p. 13. The real available seats are even less than the 70,000 figure suggests. For the 1992-93 school year, for instance, about 3,400 seats were given to the children of the martyred (those killed in the war with Iraq or in armed conflicts with the opposition). Also, 40% of the remaining seats were reserved for Pasdaran (Islamic Revolutionary Guards) and Basij. See the above source, pp. 5, 14.
95. The London-based *Economist*, October 23, 1982 gives the lower estimate, while the PMOI gives the higher estimate; cited in Ramy Nima, *The Wrath of Allah: Islamic Revolution and Reaction in Iran* (London: Pluto Pres, 1983), pp. 115, 158. The PMOI usually exaggerates figures and is regarded to be unreliable.
96. *Iran Times*, December 7, 1990.
97. Paul Lewis, "U.N. Inquiry Says Iran Still Abuses Human Rights," *New York Times*, November 19, 1989.
98. Middle East Watch, A Committee of Human Rights Watch, *Iran: Arrests of "Loyal Opposition" Politicians* (New York: June 29, 1990); idem, *Iran: Political Dissidents, Held for Over a Year, Are Reportedly Sentenced*, (New York: September 3, 1991).
99. Middle East Watch, *Guardians of Thought: Limits on Freedom of Expression in Iran.* The fundamentalists' censorship is not restricted to contemporary literary figures.
100. On Sirjani refer to: Iran Teachers Association (in exile), "Let Us Commemorate the Martyrdom of Saidi Sirjani as a Day of National Union," in *Mehregan: An Iranian Journal of Culture and Politics* vol. 3, no. 3, (Fall 1994), pp. 1-3. Also see *Iran Times*, 2 December 1994; according to Hamid Mossadeq, Sirjani's lawyer, Sirjani was "tortured everyday for six months in order to repudiate his open letter to Khamenehi."
101. Thomas Sancton, "The Tehran Connection: An Exclusive Look at How Iran Hunts Down Its Opponents Abroad," *Time Magazine*, March 21, 1994; Louise Lief and Richard Z. Chesnoff, "Freeing Hostages, Hiring Hit Squads," *US News & World Report*, October 7, 1991.
102. The interview was conducted on March 8, 1997. The CBS program "60 Minutes" broadcast excerpts of the interview on March 23, 1997. The entire interview was broadcast on C-SPAN on March 26, 1997.
103. *Iran Times*, April 18, 1997.

104. For an excellent account see Amir Kavian, *Mardi Ke Az Tarikh Amad*, for the biographies of Darush and Parvaneh Forouhar. Darush Forouhar was stabbed 40 times and Parvaneh was stabbed 25 times by the agents of the Ministry of Intelligence.

105. Rahnema and Nomani, *The Secular Miracle: Religion, Politics and Economic Policy in Iran* pp. 193-201; Joyce N. Wiley, "Kho'i, Abol-Qasem," in *The Oxford Encyclopedia of the Modern Islamic World*, vol. 2, ed., John L. Esposito, p. 423.

106. The major political parties, INF, LMI supported cease-fire after the liberation of Khorramshahr. It is believed that even some fundamentalists wanted to stop the war at that moment. The only main person who insisted to continue the war was Khomeini himself.

107. Shahrough Akhavi argues that Najafi was the only grand ayatollah who supported Khomeini's notion of *Velayat Faqih*. My own research casts some doubt on Najafi's support. Akhavi, "Clerical Politics in Iran Since 1979," in *The Iranian Revolution and the Islamic Republic*, eds., Keddie and Hooglund, p. 62.

108. Personal interview with Dr. Alireza Nurizadeh, London, 4 February 1995, tape #1. Dr. Nurizadeh was the editor of *Khalq Mosalman*, the organ of the Islamic People's Republican Party, which was organized by supporters of Shariatmadari.

109. Amnesty International, *Human Rights Violations against Shi'a Religious Leaders and their Followers*, June 1997.

110. See the report by AFP on July 19, 2001. The report is accessed at: <www.iranmania.com/news/currentaffairs/july01/190701f.asp>.

111. Cited in Afsaneh Najmabadi, *"Fazayh Tang Nasazegari: Zan Irani Dar Daheh Enghelab"* [Any Space for Difference?: Iranian Women in the Decade of Revolution], *Nimeye Digar: Persian Language Feminist Journal*, no. 11 (Spring 1990), p. 25.

112. Makroh means strongly discouraged, although not absolutely prohibited.

113. See Eliz Sanasarian, "An Analysis of Fida'i and Mujahidin Positions on Women's Rights," in *Women and Revolution in Iran*, ed. Guity Nashat, p. 103. According to Sanasarian and others girls as young as **nine** years-old were executed.

114. For some of the internal discussions on this matter see the political diaries of Ayatollah Montazeri who was Khomeini's successor during that period. Ayatollah HusseinAli Montazeri, *Khaterat*, pp. 350-351 in the version published by Ketab Corporation. Also see the passage in Ayatollah Montazeri's web site: <www.Montazeri.com> Chapter 10, section "Emphasis on Prohibiting the Execution of Apostate Women and Girls."

115. Suroosh Irfani, *Iran's Islamic Revolution: Popular Liberation or Religious Dictatorship?*, pp. 266-267; Ramy Nima, *The Wrath of Allah*, p. 113; Shaul Bakhash, *The Reign of the Ayatollahs*, p. 221; and personal interviews with several former political prisoners.

116. Irfani, op. cit., pp. 266-267.

117. For an account of this episode in English see Sanasarian, *The Women's Rights Movement in Iran*, p. 147.

118. Cited in Nima, *The Wrath of Allah*, p. 113.

119. *Iran Times*, September 25, 1981, cited in Bakhash, op. cit., p. 221.

120. *Iran Times*, July 15, 1994, pp. 1, 14, and in the English section.

121. Ibid.

122. See *Iran Times*, December 16, 1994, p. 12.

123. Ali Banuazizi, "Social-Psychological Approaches to Political Development," in *Understanding Political Development*, eds. Weiner and Huntington, pp. 307-8. The words in the parentheses are by Banuazizi.

124. Friedl, "State Ideology and Village Women," in *Women and Revolution in Iran*, ed. Nashat, p. 224.

NOTES TO CHAPTER 3

1.   There are a large number of works that provide a comprehensive summary of various feminist theories; cf. Rosemarie Tong, *Feminist Thought: A Comprehensive Introduction*; Alison Jaggar and Paula Rothenberg Struhl, eds., *Feminist Frameworks: Alternative Theoretical Accounts of the Relations between Women and Men*, 1st and 2nd editions; Margaret L. Andersen, *Thinking About Women: Sociological Perspectives on Sex and Gender* 2nd edition.

2.   John Stuart Mill and Harriet Mill argue against those who were for continued female lack of the right to vote, to education, to manage and own property. See *Essays on Sex Equality*, edited and with an introduction by Alice S. Rossi.

3.   Haleh Afshar, "Khomeini's Teachings and their Implications for Iranian Women," in *In the Shadow of Islam: The Women's Movement in Iran*, eds. Tabari and Yeganeh, pp. 77-79. Analogies between Islamic fundamentalism and fascism abound not only on gender issues but also in other spheres. See Eliz Sanasarian, "The Politics of Gender and Development in the Islamic Republic of Iran," in *Journal of Developing Societies*, p. 61; Said Amir Arjomand, *The Turban for the Crown*; Mansoor Moaddel, *Class, Politics, and Ideology in the Iranian Revolution*.

4.   Farah Azari, "Sexuality and Women's Oppression in Iran," in *Women of Iran: The Conflict with Fundamentalist Islam*, ed. Azari, pp. 90-156.

5. Cited in Valentine Moghadam, "Introduction: Women and Identity Politics in Theoretical and Comparative Perspective," in *Identity Politics and Women: Cultural Reassertions and Feminisms in International Perspective*, ed. Moghadam, p. 18.
6. Ibid.
7. Rafsanjani's Friday Prayer sermon on Farvardin 15, 1365, cited in Afsaneh Najmabadi, "Any Space For Differences?" in *Nimeye Digar: Persian Language Feminist Journal*, no. 11, Spring 1990, p. 30, (in Farsi).
8. Sanasarian, *The Women's Rights Movement in Iran*, p. 155.
9. Some scholars such as Sanasarian argue that there are no significant differences on gender issues among these forces. According to Sanasarian, "Individuals such as Prime Minister Mehdi Bazargan and President Bani Sadr, despite being termed as politically liberal or moderate, were neither when it came to gender policy. In fact, most of the restrictive measures against women were launched during the first three years. They included profound changes in family laws to the clear disadvantage of women, forced hejab, and restrictions on women's choices of work. Why did the new elite, despite severe conflicts and power struggle, express such unanimity on issues involving gender relations?" See Sanasarian, "The Politics of Gender and Development in the Islamic Republic of Iran," p. 58. Many other scholars argue that there are wide and conflicting views on gender among various Islamic ideologies. On differences between Islamic fundamentalists and Islamic modernists refer to Adele Ferdows, "Women in the Iranian Revolution," in *IJMES*, vol. 15, no. 2, May 1983; Roy Andersen et al., *Politics and Change in the Middle East: Sources of Conflict and Accommodation*, third edition, pp. 279-286. My own views are similar to the latter sources.
10. On women Islamic fundamentalist groups and ideologies see the seminal article by Eliz Sanasarian, "Political Activism and Islamic Identity in Iran," in *Women in the World: 1975-1985 The Women's Decade*, second revised edition, eds. Lynne Iglitzin and Ruth Ross, pp. 207-223. On Schlafly and American anti-feminists refer to Zillah Eisenstein, *Feminism and Sexual Equality: Crisis in Liberal America*. On the charge that feminism leads to disillusionment, misery and loneliness see Susan Faludi, "Backlash," in *Feminism in Our Time: The Essential Writings, World War II to the Present*, ed. Miriam Schneir, pp. 454-468.
11. For reviews of Iranian fundamentalist views on women refer to: Nahid Yeganeh, "Women's Struggles in the Islamic Republic of Iran," in *In the Shadow of Islam: The Women's Movement in Iran*, eds. Azar Tabari and Nahid Yeganeh, pp. 26-74; Eliz Sanasarian, "Political Activism and Islamic Identity in Iran." On American anti-feminism refer to Zillah Eisenstein, "Antifeminism and the New Right," and Jan Rosenberg, "Feminism, the

Family, and the New Right," both in *Class, Race, and Sex: The Dynamics of Control*, eds. Swerdlow and Lessinger.

12. Dr. Schlafly's statement before a U.S. Senate labor subcommittee in 1981, quoted in *Los Angeles Herald Examiner*, April 22, 1981, p. 2, cited in Steffen W. Schmidt et al., *American Government and Politics Today*, 1993-1994 edition, p. 184.

13. Jerry Falwell, *Listen America*, p. 148, cited in Zillah Eisenstein, "Antifeminism and the New Right," p. 121.

14. Afsaneh Najmabadi, "Hazards of Modernity and Morality: Women, State and Ideology in Contemporary Iran," in *Women, Islam and the State*, ed. Deniz Kandiyoti, p. 50.

15. Ayatollah Morteza Mottahari, *Women's Rights in Islam*, cited in Minou Reeves, *Female Warriors of Allah: Women and the Islamic Revolution*, pp. 177f.

16. Haleh Afshar, "Women, State and Ideology," in *Third World Quarterly*, vol. 17, no. 2, April 1985.

17. Quoted in *Iran Liberation*, #144, November 16, 1984, p. 4, cited in Rokhsareh S. Shoaee, "The Mujahid Women of Iran: Reconciling 'Culture' and 'Gender'," in *The Middle East Journal*, vol. 41, no. 4, Autumn, 1987, pp. 521-2.

18. Eliz Sanasarian, "The Politics of Gender and Development in the Islamic Republic of Iran," p. 59. Willem M. Floor, "The Revolutionary Character of the Iranian Ulama," p. 509.

19. Willem Floor, "The Revolutionary Character of the Iranian Ulama," p. 510.

20. Cited in Rahnema and Nomani, *The Secular Miracle*, p. 302.

21. Quoted in Amir Kabir, *Dar Josteju-ye Rah*, p. 15, cited in Shoaee, "The Mujahid Women of Iran," pp. 522, 524.

22. See the Appendix in Willem Floor, "The Revolutionary Character of the Iranian Ulama," p. 524.

23. "The Role of Women after the Revolution," in *Mahjubah*, 1, no. 9, November-December 1981, p. 9, cited in Patricia J. Higgins, "Women in the Islamic Republic of Iran: Legal, Social, and Ideological Changes," in *Signs*, vol. 10, no. 3, 1985, p. 492.

24. *Zan-e Rouz*, April 7, 1984, cited and translated in Afsaneh Najmabadi, "Hazards of Modernity and Morality: Women, State and Ideology in Contemporary Iran," p. 67.

25. The image of Eve, especially as portrayed in the Hadith (the sayings and traditions of the Prophet Mohammed), is identical to that of the Judeo-Christian myths. On this point see Jane Smith and Yvonne Haddad, "Eve: Islamic Image of Woman," in *Women's Studies International Forum*, vol. 5, no. 2.

26. Cited in Najmabadi, "Hazards of Modernity," p. 68.

27. *Edwardsville Intelligencer*, March 5, 1994, pp. 1, 12.

28. *Iran Times*, October 8, 1993, p. 1. Hojatolislam Abbasi's words were uttered in the Majles in opposition to the creation of a special committee on women.

29. Afshar, "Women, State and Ideology," in *Third World Quarterly*, vol. 17, no. 2, April 1985.

30. Lisa Desposito, "The New Right and the Abortion Issue," in *Class, Race, and Sex*, p. 144.

31. Bradwell v. Illinois, 1873, Concurring Opinion by Justice Bradley, also concurred by two other justices.

32. For Mary Wollstonecraft and Abigail Adams see their views in *Feminism: The Essential Historical Writings*, ed. Miriam Schneir, pp. 2-16; for the Mills refer to John Stuart Mill and Harriet Taylor Mill, *Essays on Sex Equality*, ed. Alice S. Rossi.

33. By "sex," I refer to a biologically determined characteristic; that is male and female. By "gender," I refer to socially constructed notions of masculinity and femininity (and in many cultures various shades thereof) which are different in various societies.

34. Cited in Steffen W. Schmidt et al., *American Government and Politics*, 1993-1994 edition, p. 182.

35. This debate on nature vs. nurture is far more complicated than the sketch I have presented here. See Andersen, *Thinking About Women* for a more complete treatment of the subject.

36. Virginia Woolf, *Three Guineas*; Carol Gilligan, *In a Different Voice: Psychological Theory and Women's Development*; Judith Stiehm, her lectures in a class in which I was her teaching assistant.

37. See Andersen. John Stuart Mill's and Harriet Taylor Mill's basic arguments, despite their time distance, are not outdated on this issue.

38. Nayereh Tohidi, *Zan va Gheshriyoun Islami* (Women and Fundamentalism In Contemporary Iran), in Farsi. In the words of Maryam Behrouzi--an official in the fundamentalist women's group and a member of Majles--"the greatest treason which today's world does to women is to separate their children from warm embrace and deprive their laps of building valuable people. Nursery schools, kindergartens and day care centers build machine-like people"; she further added that Islamic rules are against abortion and sterilization; refer to Tabari and Yeganeh, p. 239. On attributing day-care centers to imperialism see Najmabadi, "Hazards of Modernity and Morality," p. 69.

39. For details on these groups refer to Azar Tabari and Nahid Yeganeh, eds. *In the Shadow of Islam*, pp. 141-2, 227-9. Both translations of "Liberation Movement of Iran" and "Freedom Movement of Iran" have been used for "Nehzat Azadi Iran," which is the largest liberal Islamist party in Iran.

40. The document compiled in Tabari and Yeganeh, *In the Shadow of Islam*, p. 228.
41. Document compiled in Tabari and Yeganeh, *In the Shadow of Islam*, pp. 141-2.
42. The Freedom Movement (also translated as the Liberation Movement of Iran) was founded by Mehdi Bazargan and Ayatollah Mahmud Taleghani in 1961. The Freedom Movement was the quintessential Islamic modernist group in Iran. See Chehabi, *Iranian Politics and Religious Modernism*.
43. There is a debate whether or not Marx's views are similar to those of Engels. Avineri in *The Social and Political of Karl Marx* argues in the negative. I agree with Hal Draper (in *Karl Marx's Theory of Revolution*, vol. 1) and Michele Barrett (Introduction to Engels, *The Origin of the Family, Private Property and the State*) that although their views were not completely identical, they were nevertheless extremely close.
44. Susan Himmelweit, "The Real Dualism of Sex and Class," in *Review of Radical Political Economics*, vol. 16, no. 1, Spring 1984, p. 169.
45. Lenin's praise is typical, "This is one of the fundamental works of modern socialism, every sentence of which can be accepted with confidence, in the assurance that it has not been said at random but is based on immense historical and political material." Lenin, *Collected Works*, vol. 30, p. 473, cited by Michele Barrett in the "Introduction" to Engels, *The Origins of the Family, Private Property and the State*, p. 13. All references of Engels' work are to this edition.
46. Zillah R. Eisenstein (ed.), *Capitalist Patriarchy and the Case for Socialist Feminism*, p. 18.
47. Engels, op. cit., pp. 35-36; emphases are mine.
48. "The modern individual family is founded on the open or concealed domestic slavery of the wife, and modern society is a mass composed of these individual families as its molecules. ...Within the family he is the bourgeois, and the wife represents the proletariat. ...Then [after complete legal equality of rights] it will be plain that the **first** condition for the liberation of the wife is to bring the whole female sex back into public industry, and that this in turn demands that the characteristic unit of society be abolished." Engels, OP. cit., p. 105, the phrase in the bracket is mine.
49. Eisenstein, *Capitalist Patriarchy*, pp. 1-40; and Heidi Hartmann, "The Unhappy Marriage Of Marxism and Feminism: Towards A More Progressive Union," in *Women and Revolution: A Discussion of the Unhappy Marriage of Marxism and Feminism*, ed. Lydia Sargent.
50. For the relationships between patriarchy, sex-segregated labor market and socialism refer to Roslyn L. Feldberg, "Women, Self-Management, and Socialism," in *Socialist Review*, vol. 56, 1981, pp. 141-152; also see Heidi Hartmann, "Capitalism, Patriarchy, and Job Segregation by Sex," in *Signs*,

vol. 1, no. 3, part 2, Spring 1976, pp. 137-169.

51. A case in point would be the position of women in the former USSR and other former Communist nations.
52. Engels, op. cit., p. 96. Also see Marx, *The Philosophical and Economic Manuscripts*.
53. Here "bourgeois woman" refers to the wives and daughters of bourgeois man, not those rare females who own and control the major means of production directly.
54. Refer to Tabari and Yeganeh, op. cit., pp. 143-170, 201-227.
55. For comprehensive reviews of this subject refer to: Hammed Shahidian, "The Iranian Left and the 'Woman Question' in the Revolution of 1978-79," in *IJMES*, vol. 26, no. 2, May 1994, pp. 223-247; Soraya Afshar, "The Attitude of the Iranian Left to the Women's Question," in *Women of Iran: The Conflict with Fundamentalist Islam*, ed. Farah Azari.
56. Peykar, "Piramun Junbesh Zanan Zahmatkesh" (Concerning the Movement of the Toiling Women) part 3, in *Peykar*, #95, February 23, 1981, translated by and cited in Hammed Shahidian, "The Iranian Left," p. 238. It is imperative to add that Peykar, like other Iranian Stalinist parties, uses the term "democratic" in a particular sense. It does not refer to the right of people to vote or organize their own political parties and organizations or what is usually understood as democratic rights such as freedoms of the press, speech, assembly, etc. For Peykar, and other Stalinist groups in Iran, the term "democratic" refers to that stage which precedes socialism; in that stage the leadership of proletariat (i.e., the politburo of the said party to be more precise) is accepted by certain groups that are neither bourgeois nor proletarian but follow the dictates of the party of the proletariat (i.e., the politburo of Peykar in this case). "Democratic groups" refers to these groups which follow the lead of the party prior to and during the democratic phase preceding socialism.
57. Tabari, "Islam and the Struggle for Emancipation of Iranian Women," and Yeganeh, "Women's Struggles in the Islamic Republic of Iran," both in *In the Shadow of Islam*, eds. Tabari and Yeganeh; Soraya Afshar, "The Attitude of the Iranian Left to the Women's Question," in *Women of Iran*, ed. Azari; Tabari, "The Women's Movement in Iran: A Hopeful Prognosis," in *Feminist Studies*, vol. 12, no. 2, Summer 1986; Sanasarian, "An Analysis of Fida'i and Mujahidin Positions on Women's Rights," in *Women and Revolution in Iran*, ed. Nashat.
58. Democratic Organization of Iranian Women, *My Struggle Is My Work*, pp. 7-8, cited in Hammed Shahidian, "The Iranian Left," pp. 235-236. Democratic Organization of Iranian Women is the women's front group of the Tudeh.
59. Cited in Shahidian, "The Iranian Left," p. 240.

60. "Azadi Zanan as Azadi Jameh Juda Nist" (Women's Emancipation is not Separate from the Emancipation of Society) in *Kar*, #2, March 15, 1979, translated and cited in Shahidian, "The Iranian Left," p. 234. *Kar* is the organ of the Fadaian.

61. For citations refer to Shahidian, "The Iranian Left," pp. 238-241.

62. The PMOI, of course, disclaim the label "Marxist" because Marxism is atheistic. However, they refer to Marxist analyses as "knowledge" and "social science" upon which they rely extensively in their analyses. For these reasons the fundamentalists refer to the Mojahedin as *"elteghati"* (mixed-up) and *"monafeghin"* (hypocrites).

63. Masoud Rajavi, "Last Defense," at trial, 27, Bahman 1350 (Iranian calendar), 1972.

64. Masoud Rajavi, *Tabeen Jahan*, First session, Part 2, pp. 36-38.

65. Rajavi, *Tabeen Jahan*, First session, Part 2, pp. 37-38. Rajavi's emphasis on the saliency of leadership is quite amazing. For Rajavi, Stalinists who had already accepted an all-powerful leader, were not giving enough recognition to the need for powerful leaders. For Rajavi, if a society did not reach its goal, it is the fault of the leader who did not lead. Rajavi uses the analogy of ship captain in taking a ship to its destination as a model of leadership. For Rajavi, the leader determines the solutions of all contradictions, and the subservient followers could not evaluate the leader because by definition the leader is above the followers. If a follower wanted to evaluate the leader, in effect he is placing himself above the leader: and that cannot be allowed. Rajavi argues that Nabovat [prophethood] is the sort of leadership that could establish the classless society.

66. The PMOI which was under the leadership of Masoud Rajavi (inside prison) and Ahmad Rezaee and Reza Rezaee outside carried out several assassinations and assassination attempts of US personnel in Iran including Gen. Harold Price (11 Khordad 1351 Iranian calendar) who escaped death but was seriously wounded, and Col. Lewis Hawkins (12 Khordad 1352) in addition to many assassinations of the Shah's high military officers. See the description of the events by one of the top leaders of the PMOI, Mr. Tourab Hagh-Shenas in: <www.didgah.com/didgah/aweek/1380/week17/ mon/ Sho hada.pdf>. The address of the archives of Paykar could be ordered from: Andeesheh va Paykar, Postfach 600132, 60331 Frankfurt, Germany. In 1975, the majority of the members and leaders of the PMOI abandoned Islam and declared themselves to be Marxist-Leninist and followed the path of Maoism. The Marxist-Leninist PMOI continued with assassinations of American personnel. In 1979, the changed their name to Paykar..Those who had remained Muslim, kept the name PMOI and were led by Masoud Rajavi. The PMOI in the period February 1979 to 1983 continued to be the most virulently anti-American group in Iran, and supported the taking of American

Embassy personnel hostage and condemned those who tried to release them. In the mid-1980s, after the PMOI was defeated by the fundamentalists, Rajavi escaped to France. From about 1983-84, the PMOI decided to get support from the US government in its struggle against the fundamentalist regime. The US State Department has refused to support the PMOI and has classified it as a "terrorist organization." As part of the evidence, the State Department mentions the Islamic PMOI's assassinations of American personnel in the early 1970s. Strangely, the PMOI publicly lies and claims that it has not assassinated the American personnel and they were assassinated by the Marxist "infiltrators."

67. The PMOI, *Erteja Chist? va Mortaje Kist?* [What is Reaction? and Who is Reactionary?] This PMOI publication published in July 1980 gathered the articles from "Mojahed" in one pamphlet. The three quotes cited are in pages 27, 28, and 29.
68. Communication with numerous affiliates of the PMOI. In addition, see Peter Waldman, "Fading Force: Anti-Iran Guerrillas Lose Disciples but Gain Friends in Washington," in *Wall Street Journal*, October 4, 1994. Also discussions with Ervand Abrahamian, who is one of the foremost experts on the PMOI and Iranian modern history.
69. Cited in Peter Waldman, op. cit.
70. The analysis of the Mojahedin in the following pages is relevant for the organization in the 1979-1984 period. There has occurred a major transformation of the Mojahedin from a mass-based left party into what Abrahamian calls a "cult" dominated by a cult of personality. In the 1990s, the Mojahedin have been seeking financial and political support from the U.S. government in their attempts to overthrow the fundamentalists. Moreover, the Mojahedin abandoned their socialist and anti-imperialist slogans and analyses in the mid- to late 1980s. Interestingly, the Mojahedin have emphasized and publicized their policies promoting equality between men and women although it would be problematic to refer to these later emphases on gender equality as Marxist feminism. See Ervand Abrahamian, *The Iranian Mojahedin*, and Peter Waldman, "Fading Force, Anti-Iran Guerrillas Lose Disciples but Gain Friends in Washington; Mujahdeen Khalq, in Iraq, Claims to Be Democratic But Suppresses Dissent: Beatings, Jailings, Divorces," in *The Wall Street Journal*, October 4, 1994, pp. 1, 6.
71. See Mojahedin, "On the Question of Hejab," and Fadaian (Minority), "Compulsory Veiling Under the Pretext of Fighting Imperialist Culture," both in *In the Shadow of Islam*, pp. 126-129; the Mojahedin statement was issued on March 12, 1979, and the Fadaian's in early summer of 1980.
72. PMOI, "On the Question of Hejab," in *In the Shadow of Islam*, p. 126.

73. See PMOI, "On the Question of Hejab," and Fadaian-Minority, "Compulsory Veiling Under the Pretext of Fighting Imperialist Culture," both in *In the Shadow of Islam*, pp. 126-129.
74. There are two verses in the Koran which "Islamic feminists" draw upon in their arguments that in "true" Islam, men and women are equal (these two verses are cited by the Mojahedin pamphlet which is quoted here). There are other verses where the Koran explicitly states that men are superior to women. The latter verses are usually ignored by "Islamic feminists" and emphasized by secular feminists who regard Islam to be patriarchal and misogynist.
75. Mojahedin, *Women on the Path of Liberation*, translated in *In the Shadow of Islam*, pp. 112-126. All the emphases are in the original. The term "tawhidi" literally means "unitary." The Mojahedin use it to connote their belief that Islam promotes and promises a class-less society which seeks a divinely inspired unity as a reflection of a unitary God.
76. See Article 3, for instance, p. 31.
77. "Article 10, Political and Social Equality between Women and Men," pp. 40f.
78. *Iran Times*, October 29, 1993, pp. 1, 12.
79. PMOI, *Amozesh va Tashrih Etelaiyh Taeen Mavazeh Sazeman Mojahedin Khalq Iran Dar Barabar Jaryan Opportunist-hay Chap-nama.* [Education and Explanation on the Declaration and Position of the PMOI on the Pseudo-Leftist Opportunist Current], (PMOI Publications: Tir 1358), (1979). The educational pamphlet #3, p. 50, footnote 1. United States Department of State, *Patterns of Global Terrorism, 1999*, April 2000, p. 80. The State Department document could be viewed at: www.state.gov/www/global/terrorism/index.html
80. Masoud Rajavi, *Tabeen Jahan*, Session 1, part 1, page 15. In referring to the taking of American diplomats hostage, Rajavi said: "It has become clear that liberation and the victory of our revolution in the first step has to go through the heart of American imperialism, and not through any other region. We have to tear apart that bad intentioned heart and go forward." The PMOI, in its march 18, 1979 "Minimum Expectation Program," stated: "The PMOI minimum-expectation program is based on the Islamic ideology, involving the Towhidi (Divinely integrated) world-view, and militates towards the negation of the political, economic, military and cultural effects of imperialism in every aspect—the imperialism which is led by the United States of America. U.S.-led imperialism is that satanic and blasphemous force which has been responsible for a greater plunder of the heritage of peoples than any other power in history." Translated in PMOI, *Mojahed: The Organ of the People's Mojahedin Organization of Iran*, vol. 1, no. 5, May 1980, p. 24. For PMOI vicious attacks on liberals who were trying to get the American diplomats released see: PMOI, "The Latest Style - Brought to You by Imperialism," in

ibid, pp. 6-7, 37.

81. PMOI, *Mojahed* (the organ of the PMOI), number 256, p. 22. Could be found in the internet at: www.golshan.com/Asnaad/Mojahed/Html/Kamal01.html. "To explain this pure moments, we have to use the culture of Quran and use equivalents with the prophets. Attributes of Rajavi cannot be described and explained except by reference to (their equivalents in) the sacrifice of Prophet Abraham, the life-giving breath of Jesus, light of guidance of the Prophet Mohammad, courage and determination of First Shia Imam Ali, and utter sacrifice of the Third Shia Imam Hussein." My translation.

82. With respect to issues such as the analysis of female subordination, the necessity of a revolution against capitalism and the ushering in of socialism as the solution to female inequality, and the goal of male and female equality, the positions of the Mojahedin and Marxist feminists are similar.

83. See Azar Tabari, "Islam and the Struggle for Emancipation of Iranian Women," in *In The Shadow of Islam*.

84. For example: (1) the Koran and Islam clearly allowed slavery, which the Mojahedin condemn; (2) the Prophet Mohammed and the Koran explicitly supported private property and therefore class society which the Mojahedin reject; (3) the Mojahedin simultaneously believe in the evolution of humans from animals and the creation of humans by God as a single divine act. There are no words in the Koran or Hadith on the evolution of humans from animals; and (4) the Quran allows polygyny and Shia Islam allows sigheh, but the PMOI oppose these practices. For the members of the PMOI, Islam is not what the Quran says or what the Prophet did and said. Rather for the PMOI affiliates, "true Islam" is what Rajavi says it is. In other words, anything in the Quran or in the deeds and sayings of the Prophet Mohammad that are contrary to the PMOI ideology and Rajavi's views, are not regarded to be the essence of Islam by the supporters of the PMOI. The PMOI members do not follow the dictates of the Quran if they contradict the policies of the PMOI.

85. Under the rubric of radical feminism, I include not only radical feminism proper but also its off-shoots: eco-feminism, spiritual feminism, and what Alice Echols calls cultural feminism. See Echols, "The New Feminism of Yin and Yang," in *Powers of Desire: The Politics of Sexuality*, eds. Snitow, Stansell and Thompson.

86. Shulamith Firestone, "The Dialectic of Sex," in Jagger and Rothenberg, op. cit., pp. 136-144; also see Charlotte Bunch, "Lesbians in Revolt," in ibid., pp. 144-148, (in her other writings Bunch seems to be closer to socialist feminists but in this article she is squarely within the radical feminist paradigm); Marilyn Frye, *The Politics of Reality: Essays in Feminist Theory*. I might be mistaken, but in my readings I have found Adrienne Rich and Mary Daly to be somewhere in between.

87. Robin Morgan, *Going Too Far*, cited in Michael Albert et al., *Liberating Theory*, p. 41.

88. See Frye, op. cit.

89. Adrienne Rich, *Of Woman Born: Motherhood as Experience and Institution*, pp. 40-41.

90. Shulamith Firestone, *The Dialectic of Sex*, excerpts in *Feminist Frameworks: Alternative Theoretical Accounts of the Relations Between Women and Men*, eds. Alison Jagger and Paula Rothenberg Struhl, pp. 120-121.

91. Shulamith Firestone, *The Dialectic of Sex*, cited in Michael Albert et al., *Liberating Theory*, p. 41; the words in brackets are by Albert et al.

92. Carol Gilligan, a liberal feminist, argues that women's rationality is **different** from that of men. Women's rationality is more relational, whereas men's is more mathematical and instrumental. Both men and women are rational but in different ways. A large number of radical feminists (such as Mary Daly, *Gyn/Ecology: The Metaethics of Radical Feminism*) believe that women are not rational. Indeed, the whole enlightenment period, they argue, was a major setback for women. Spiritual feminists and eco-feminists are whole-heartedly against rationality. They celebrate irrationality, Goddess worship, "bizarre ritualistic-shaman worship" etc. I owe this understanding to Dr. Gloria Orenstein, one of the more prominent leaders of spiritual and eco-feminism. In the semester I worked for her as a teaching assistant, I learned more about spiritual feminism than any work I had read on or by this branch of feminism. Her patience in the face of a bewildered ultra-rationalistic skeptical male cannot but be highly appreciated.

93. Ellen Willis, "The Challenge of Profamily Politics: A Feminist Defense of Sexual Freedom," in *Class, Race, and Sex: The Dynamics of Control*, eds. Swerdlow and Lessinger, p. 329.

94. Ibid. Ironically, among the lesbian community, there exist the "butch" and "femm" roles which reproduce male "predatory and sadistic" and female "victim and masochistic" status both in sexual lives and in everyday "identities."

95. Alison Jaggar et al., *Feminist Frameworks*, p. 81.

96. See the debate between Catherine MacKinnon and Floyd Abrams, moderated by Anthony Lewis, in *The New York Times Magazine*, March 13, 1994.

97. Michael Albert et al., *Liberating Theory*, pp. 162-164.

98. See Willis, op. cit., and Lillian S. Robinson, "Women, Media, and the Dialectics of Resistance," in *Class, Race, and Sex*.

99. Robinson, "Women, Media, and the Dialectics of Resistance," p. 321.

100. Margaret A. Simons, "Beauvoir and the Roots of Radical Feminism," the latest draft as of January 1993. Earlier versions of the paper were presented to: Midwest Division of the Society for Women in Philosophy, Philosophy and Women's Studies Colloquium at Loyola University, and the Society for

Phenomenolgy and Existential Philosophy. I would like to thank Professor Simons for providing me a draft of this paper and granting permission to quote from it.

101. For the law which prescribes execution for the production of pornographic videos and movies see *Iran Times*, December 31, 1993, pp. 1, 11.

102. The fundamentalist regime has gone so far as to forcefully segregate men and women in buses, queues for foodstuffs, ski slopes, swimming pools and the Caspian Sea resorts. See Rahnema and Nomani, *The Secular Miracle*, p. 221.

103. For an excellent essay that deals with these issues see: Azar Tabari, "The Women's Movement in Iran: A Hopeful Prognosis," in *Feminist Studies*, vol. 12, no. 2, (Summer 1986).

104. Mary Elain Hegland, "'Traditional' Iranian Women; How They Cope," in *The Middle East Journal*, vol. 36, no. 4, Autumn 1982, pp. 486-7.

105. Heidi Hartmann, "The Unhappy Marriage of Marxism and Feminism: Towards a More Progressive Union," in *Women and Revolution: A Discussion of the Unhappy Marriage of Marxism and Feminism*, ed. Lydia Sargent; Hartmann, "The Historical Roots of Occupational Segregation: Capitalism, Patriarchy, and Job Segregation by Sex," in *Signs*, vol. 1, no. 3, part 2, Spring 1976; Gayle Rubin, "The traffic in Women: Notes on the 'Political Economy' of Sex," in *Towards an Anthropology of Women*, ed. Rayna R. Reiter; Nancy Hartsock, "Feminist Theory and the Development of Revolutionary Strategy," in *Capitalist Patriarchy and the Case for Socialist Feminism*, ed. Zillah Eisenstein; Zillah Eisenstein, "Developing a Theory of Capitalist Patriarchy and Socialist Feminism" and "Some Notes on the Relations of Capitalist Patriarchy," both in Eisenstein, ibid.

106. Hartmann, "The Unhappy Marriage," p. 9.

107. Ibid., pp. 10-11, emphases in original.

108. Ibid., pp. 14-15.

109. Ibid., pp. 23-25.

110. Zillah Eisenstein, "Developing A Theory of Capitalist Patriarchy and Socialist Feminism," p. 5. By postcapitalist society is meant the communist polities of the former USSR, Eastern Europe, and China, Cuba, etc.

111. For an attempt in this direction in the Middle East refer to Nikki R. Keddie, "Introduction: Deciphering Middle Eastern Women's History," in *Women in Middle Eastern History: Shifting Boundaries in Sex and Gender*, eds. Nikki Keddie and Beth Baron.

112. I have borrowed this line of argument from Michael Albert et al., *Liberating Theory*, pp. 33-45.

113. Herbert Marcuse, "Socialist Feminism: The Hard Core of the Dream," in *Edcentric*, no. 31-32, November 1974, p. 7.

114. Ibid.

115. Ibid.

116. Eisenstein, "Developing a Theory of Capitalist Patriarchy and Socialist Feminism," in *Capitalist Patriarchy and the Case for Socialist Feminism*, pp. 9-10, 16, 25. For further elaboration refer to Chapter Five.

117. Personal interview with Dr. Ali Shirazi, one of the principal founders and leaders of the ULC; Santa Monica, California, 1988.

118. The ULC was Marxist, anti-Stalinist, and non-Leninist. It was composed of Iran's most celebrated independent Marxist intellectuals. Along with the "Organization of Communist Unity" it was the only Marxist party in the post-revolutionary period which advocated civil liberties (e.g., freedoms of the press, speech, assembly, etc.). Among other things, the ULC coined the term "political pluralism" for the debates among Iranian parties. In conjunction with the experience with the Islamic Republic, the ULC's ideological debates had a tremendous impact on democratizing the Iranian left and should be credited for the de-Stalinization of the Iranian left in the mid-1980s.

119. In *Payam Azadi*, no. 18, Farvardin 1362 (March 1983), in Farsi. The translation is mine. Also refer to the article "Namehee az Zanan Iran" (A Letter from Iranian Women), in *Payam Azadi*, no. 21, Mordad 1362 (August 1983). While reading this long quotation, one should keep in mind that the ULC was a Marxist group which had already produced extensive and innovative class analysis of Iran and that its primary audience was Iranian leftists. The significance and saliency of class is taken for granted, and the article is trying to bring to attention the hitherto neglected oppression of gender as gender, hence the emphasis on patriarchy.

NOTES TO CHAPTER 4

1. Koran, Surah 4, verse 34, Translated by M. H. Shakir. The translation by A. J. Arberry of this passage uses these words instead, "Men are the managers of the affairs of women, for that God has preferred in bounty one of them over another, and for that they have expended of their property. Righteous women are therefore obedient... And those you fear may be rebellious, admonish, banish them to their couches, and beat them."

2. *The Holy Qur'an*, ed. S. V. Mir Ahmed Ali, with special notes from Ayatollah Agha Haji Mirza Mahdi Pooya Yazdi, p. 374.

3. Ayatollah Pooya Yazdi, op. cit. p. 1374.

4. *Koran*, Surah 4, Verses 3, 129; Surah 33, Verses 50, 52, 53.

5. *Koran*, Surah 4, Verses 24-25; Surah 33, Verses 50, 52.

6. Ali Dashti, *23 Years: A Study of the Prophetic Career of Mohammad*, p. 125.

7. The Koran, Surah 33, Verses 50, 51, 52.

8. Nazih N. Ayubi, "Rethinking the Public/Private Dichotomy: Radical Islamism and Civil Society in the Middle East," in *Contention: Debates in Society, Culture, and Sciences*, vol. 4, no. 3 (Spring 1995), p. 88. "* Khalil 'Ali

Haidar, *Tayyarat al-sahawa al-islamiyys* [Currents in the Islamic Revival] (Kuwait: Kazima, 1987), 28-30." "** Sa'id Hawwa, *Jund Allah* [God's Soldiers] (Cairo: n.p., c. 1980), 324."

9. See for example, the many verses in Surah 2. Nowhere is God addressing women in these verses. In other words "you" always refers to men, and "them" always to women. It is important to add that the Koran is basically addressed to men. There are passages, however, that it specifically addresses women.

10. The two verses are Surah 4, Verses 35 and 128. These two verses say that judges may be chosen to arbitrate between the husband and wife. They do not say a word about women's right to divorce. However, some schools of thought have created rules under which a religious judge may grant women a divorce.

11. The emphases are mine.

12. The words in the brackets are mine. In the Koran, God is primarily speaking to males. "You" usually refers to males and "they" usually refers to females. When God is directly speaking to women, usually after "you" the word "women" is added or is present in the verse.

13. Nawal El Saadawi, "Women and Islam," and Azizah Al-Hibri, "A Study of Islamic Herstory: Or How Did We Ever Get Into This Mess?" both in *Women's Studies International Forum*, vol. 5, no. 2, 1982; Azar Tabari, "The Rise of Islam: What Did Happen to Women?" in *Khamsin*, op. cit.; Deniz Kandiyoti, "Islam and Patriarchy: A Comparative Perspective," and Leila Ahmed, "Early Islam and the Position of Women: The Problem of Interpretation," both in *Women in Middle Eastern History: Shifting Boundaries in Sex and Gender*, eds. Nikki Keddie and Beth Baron; Leila Ahmed, *Women and Gender in Islam*; Fatima Mernissi, *Beyond the Veil: Male-Female Dynamics in Modern Muslim Society* (1975; 1987); idem, *The Veil and the Male Elite: A Feminist Interpretation of Women's Rights in Islam* (1987; 1991); Farah Azari, "Islam's Appeal to Women in Iran: Illusions and Reality," and idem, "Sexuality and Women's Oppression in Iran," both in *Women of Iran: The Conflict with Fundamentalist Islam*, ed. Azari.

14. Mernissi, *Beyond the Veil*; Tabari, "The Rise of Islam"; Azari, "Islam's Appeal to Women in Iran: Illusions and Reality"; Saadawi, "Women and Islam."

15. It is important to add that Khadijeh was only one among many women who were successful merchants in pre-Islamic Arabia; Saadawi, "Women and Islam."

16. Cited in Farah Azari, "Islam's Appeal to Women in Iran," p. 9.

17. Mernissi, *Beyond the Veil*, esp. pp. 65-85.

18. When she proposed, Khadijeh was 40 years old and Mohammed was only 25.

136 *Islamic Fundamentalism, Feminism, and Gender Inequality*

19. Indeed, Mohammed was her employee. It is important to note that many years after his marriage to Khadijeh, Mohammed declared that he received the call to become the Prophet of Allah. Also important is the fact that as long as Khadijeh was alive Mohammed remained monogamous. Only after her death, when Mohammed had become a Prophet, a political leader, and wealthy, did he engage in polygyny.

20. It is noteworthy to mention that in post-revolutionary Iran, a man and a woman who engage in intercourse outside marriage are given 100 lashes. If the woman is already married she is stoned to death.

21. Mernissi, *Beyond the Veil*, pp. 65-71.

22. Cited in Mernissi, *Beyond the Veil*, pp. 67-70.

23. Farah Azari, "Sexuality and Women's Oppression in Iran," pp. 102-104.

24. Cited in Mernissi, *Beyond the Veil*, p. 70.

25. Mohammad-Ali Khalili, *Zendegani Hazrat Ali Alayhe al-Salam Amir-al-Momenin*, p.406-407. Imam Ali married numerous wives after the deaths of Prophet Mohammad and Fatima. The following list of 8 wives is compiled by Khalili. The wives of Imam Ali include: Kholeh, Ommalbenin, Ismaa Bint Amiss, Omm Sa'ad, Sahiyeh, Emameh, Omm Habibeh, Leili. Kholeh was the daughter of Iyas Ben Jaafar Hanifeh. Ommalbenin was the daughter of Haram Ibn Khaled Ibn Rabiyea Kalbieh. Ismaa Bint Amiss was the wive of Jaafar Bin Abitaleb, and after the death of Jaafar, she married Abu Bakr and gave birth to their son Mohammad, and after the death of Abu Bakr, she [Ismaa Bint Amiss] married Imam Ali. Ismaa's mother was Hend Harsieh. Hend Harsieh had 6 daughters from two husbands. Among Hend Harsieh's sons-in-law are the Prophet Mohammad, Abu Bakr, and Imam Ali. Omm Sa'ad was the daughter of Arotibn Masoud Saghafi. Sahiyeh was the daughter of Ebad Ibn Rabieh Taghlibi. Emameh was the daughter of Abol-Aaus and her mother was Zeinat [Zeinat was the daughter of the Prophet Mohammad and half-sister of Fatima]. Omm Habibeh was the daughter of Rabieh. Leili was the daughter of Masoud Ibn Khaled Tameimi who bore Imam Ali a child. Khalili mentions that others have given the names of other wives of Imam Ali, but he only mentions the above names. This book by Khalili is published in the Islamic Republic of Iran.

26. Ali's words, translated by and cited in Azari, "Sexuality and Women's Oppression in Iran," p. 103.

27. Saadawi, "Women and Islam," esp. p. 194. Also see Azizah Al-Hibri, "A Study of Islamic Herstory: Or How Did we Ever Get into This Mess?" in *Women's Studies International Forum*, vol. 5, no. 2, 1982; Mernissi, *Beyond the Veil*, p. 66.

28. Mernissi, *Beyond the Veil*, pp. 52-53, 186, note 15. Asma Bint al-Numan and Mulaika are two of the women who divorced the Prophet.

29. Cited in Mernissi, *Beyond the Veil*, p. 71. The words in brackets are by Mernissi.

30. Some "apologists" constantly reiterate that the Koran and the Prophet himself were against patriarchy and advocated complete equality of men and women but that it was the works of the Ulama and the later commentaries which were unalterably patriarchal and that they have intentionally **distorted** the meaning of the Koran and the Hadith to benefit men. A good example of this genre is Al-Hibri's statement "It seems rather evident that the whole issue of polygamy is the result of patriarchal attempts to distort the Qur'an in the male's favour." Azizah Al-Hibri, "A Study of Islamic Herstory," op. cit., p. 217. Also see John L. Esposito, "Introduction: Women in Islam and Muslim Societies," in *Islam, Gender, and Social Change*, eds., Yvonne Yazbeck Haddad and John L. Esposito, esp. xii-xiii.

31. See the cited works by Saadawi, Al-Hibri, Tabari (Najmabadi), Kandiyoti, Ahmed, Mernissi, and Azari; also see Jane Smith and Yvonne Haddad, "Eve: Islamic Image of Women," and Nazirah Zein Ed-Din, "Removing the Veil and Veiling," (translated by Salah-Dine Hammoud) both in *Women's Studies International Forum*, vol. 5, no. 2, 1982. This debate is influenced by the political situation which these scholars confront. Some seem to believe that the best way to confront the fundamentalists is to cite verses in the Koran and the Hadith which are helpful for gender equality and inimical to the commentaries (e.g., Mernissi 1991, and Ahmed). The position of Iranian feminists--like Tabari and Azari who have experienced first-hand the defeat of anti-fundamentalist Islamist groups in Iran--is premised on the notion that it is futile to try to be more Islamic than the clerics and the fundamentalists, and argue that Islam is in essence misogynist and patriarchal. Saadawi's position is closer to Tabari's but Saadawi argues that although the position of women was higher in the pre-Islamic era she also argues that the Prophet did more for women's rights than his male contemporaries. Mernissi's earlier work (*Beyond the Veil*) is closer to the position of Tabari and Azari but her later work (*The Veil and the Male Elite*) is closer to that of Saadawi. I should also mention that the issue of personal safety might be relevant here. In other words, these analyses are not innocent of political and safety considerations. Tabari (the pseudonym of Afsaneh Najmabadi) lives in the U.S. and teaches in American universities, and Azari lives in United Kingdom whereas Mernissi lives and teaches in Morocco and Saadawi in Egypt. Indeed, shortly after the final proofreading of the article mentioned earlier she was imprisoned (along with progressives and Islamists) by President Sadat in August 1981. Fundamentalist leaders easily issue fatvas condemning to death people who criticize Islam. For example, Taslimeh Nasreen, a feminist writer (and physician) from Bangladesh was condemned to death for "insulting the sacreds of Islam" by a cleric named Nasr Al-Islam; apparently her crime was

a statement in an interview in which she was quoted as saying that the Koran "should be completely revised." In a letter to the Speaker of the Parliament, Nasreen stated that "Not even one word of the Koran can be altered. I am fully aware of this issue and have never said anything on it.... The newspaper reporter [from the Indian journal] did not understand the differentiation between the Koran and Shariah. I called for changes in Shariah so that quality of rights would be guaranteed for men and women." See *Iran Times*, June 17, 1994, pp. 6, 12.

NOTES TO CHAPTER 5

1. Personal interviews. Both these incidents occurred in 1992, which is regarded as one of the least repressive periods.
2. By "historical Shiism," I refer to beliefs and practices of Shia Islam prior to contemporary alterations and reinterpretation by the various groups. I use the term "historical Shiism" in order to be able to distinguish it from the recent interpretations by the fundamentalists, Mojahedin, Bazargan, Bani Sadr and Shariati.
3. Ali Shariati, *Fatima Fatima Ast*, (Fatima is Fatima); and Mernissi, *Beyond the Veil*, pp. 51-58. On Mohammed's sexual relations with his "beautiful" Jewish and Christian concubines and the jealousy it generated among his wives see Mernissi, p. 55.
4. Dashti, op. cit., pp. 125-126.
5. *Iran Times*, December 24, 1993, pp. 1, 12. Hojatolislam Abbasi was talking in the Majles and the occasion was his opposition to the "un-Islamic atmosphere against polygamy that was being created in Iran." The text of his talk in the Majles proceeding is as follows, "Can I talk about polygyny now? Who has said that the best man is the one who spends all his life with one woman? Why are we creating such an atmosphere? The Prophet of Islam had eight wives and kept all of them in one house."
6. Cited in Mernissi, *Beyond the Veil*, p. 54.
7. Mernissi, *Beyond the Veil*, pp. 54-55.
8. Mernissi, *Beyond the Veil*, p. 55.
9. Mernissi, *Beyond the Veil*, pp. 54-58. The Prophet asked Dubaa's son to marry his mother when he heard that she was "among the most beautiful of Arab women.... Her hair was long enough to cover all her body." Apparently, after hearing that she was also aging, the Prophet did not pursue the matter any further.
10. Azar Tabari, "The Rise of Islam,"; Mernissi, *Beyond the Veil*.
11. Some versions indicate that she was taking a bath, while others maintain that she was not fully dressed and was walking around the house, when the Prophet who was her first cousin, walked into the house.

12. Koran, Surah 33, Verse 5. From Surah 33, Verse 37, it is clear that the Prophet feared the reaction of the Arab community. The Prophet had initially concealed his feelings for Zaid's wife. Surah 33, Verse 37 states: "...and you [the Prophet Mohammad] concealed in your soul what Allah would bring to light, and you feared men..."

13. Surah 33, Verses 8, 24, 25, 36, 60, 61, 64, 66, 68, 73. Verse 64 says: "Surely Allah has cursed the unbelievers and has prepared for them a burning fire."

14. The next verse goes on and says: "There is no harm in the Prophet doing that which Allah has ordained for him...."

15. Surah 4, Verse 3.

16. Cited in Mernissi, *Beyond the Veil*, p. 55.

17. Cited in Mernissi, *Beyond the Veil*, p. 55.

18. Surah 66, Verses 1-2.

19. Surah 66, Verse 5. The Shias intensely hate Ayesha despite the fact that she remained the Prophet's favorite wife and according to popular belief the Prophet died in her arms. Some Shias on religious occasions take a red-haired female kid (baby goat) which is symbolic for the red-haired Ayesha and kick and torture it extensively. This occurs at the same ceremony which the Second Caliph, Umar, is burned in effigy. Interview with Y. Gh., Toronto, Canada, August 21, 1994.

20. Surah 66, Verses 9-10.

21. Cited in Mernissi, *Beyond the Veil*, p. 50. The words in the bracket are mine.

22. The same passage mentions that in Heaven these eternally young boys are among many other amenities including: wine, fruits, chicken, and houris (beautiful women with eyes like pearl) and eternally virgin girls. Koran, (Surah al-Vaqia) Surah 56, Verses 12-22. The same description of Heaven is repeated in (Surah al-Dahr) Surah 76, Verses 19-24. The verses explicitly mentioning the "mokhalladoun" (eternally youthful boys) are 56:17, and 76:19.

23. Ibid. Fundamentalists are very uncomfortable with these verses and have re-interpreted them to mean that these "eternally youthful boys" are for the sexual enjoyment of women. This interpretation is an innovation and runs counter to the standard interpretation which has existed for over 14 centuries. It is imperative to add that in contemporary Iran, very few individuals are familiar with these verses. The debate on these verses is off limits for the public.

24. Shahla Haeri, "The Institution of Mut'a Marriage in Iran: A Formal and Historical Perspective," in *Women and Revolution in Iran*, ed. by Guity Nashat. Shahla Haeri, "Temporary Marriage and the State in Iran," op. cit. Guity Nashat, "Women in the Ideology of the Islamic Republic," in *Women and Revolution in Iran*. Ayatollah Khomeini, *Tozih al-Masael* (Explanation of Problems), Problems 2428-2439. Personal observation, Mashhad, in the

vicinity of the Eighth Imam's Shrine, 1977.

25. Haeri, "The Institution of Mut'a Marriage in Iran." Haeri further adds that because these women are non-marriageable (due to the fact that they are not virgins after their first marriages) some also engage in sigheh in order to satisfy their sexual desires.

26. Interview with Y. Gh., Toronto, Canada, August 21, 1994.

27. Cited in Afshar, "Women, State and Ideology."

28. Shahla Haeri, "Temporary Marriage and the State in Iran: An Islamic Discourse on Female Sexuality," in *Social Research*, vol. 59, no. 1, Spring 1992, p. 209.

29. For a large fee, Shia clerics can pronounce a mass sigheh declaring all the men and women in a gathering "mahram" for each other. "Mahram" is an Islamic concept which refers to those males and females who can intermingle without the necessary hejab (i.e., siblings, parents/children, spouses). Since 1985 many upper-class and upper-middle class families pay a cleric for this service in order to secure permission for males and females to intermingle in weddings without the veil. In addition, if a large sum is given as a bribe to the local Islamic Revolutionary Guards, music and dancing would also be tolerated.

30. Afsaneh Najmabadi, "Any Space for Differences?" in *Nimeye Digar: Persian Language Feminist Journal*, no. 11, Spring 1990, esp. pp. 15-18; Najmabadi's insightful article analyzes the pressures that young girls are subjected to by fundamentalist public policy. In Malayer--a small town--in one month alone, 12 young boys and girls committed suicide, see *Iran Times*, October 30, 1992, p. 13. A government report indicates that in 1993, in the province of Khorasan 1,070 males and 2,530 females committed suicide; most of these were quite young; see *Iran Times*, July 29, 1994, p. 11.

31. Nora Boustany, "In Iran, The Chador Cloaks A Growing Mood of Unrest: Women are unveiling views about their rights," in *The Washington Post National Weekly Edition*, November 2-8, 1992, p. 18.

32. Boustany, op. cit.

33. In order to avoid prosecution by the government the professor asked the *Washington Post* reporter not to disclose her name. The reporter had talked to the professor at the Symposium on Achievement Motivation for Women (organized by Khomeini's daughter, Ms. Zahra Mostafavi). Boustany, op. cit.

34. Nora Boustany, op. cit.; "On the Situation of Iranian Women: A Report from Iran," in *Payam-e Azadi*, no. 21, Mordad 1362, organ of the United Left Council, (in Farsi), p. 3.

NOTES TO CHAPTER 6

1. The extreme misogynist policies of Khomeini and fundamentalists in Iran, have compelled a large number of Iranians (particularly women) to convert to Protestant Christianity for the first time in Iranian history. Therefore, the discussion in this section is not only an academic one but one with great political significance.
2. Koran, Surah 4, Verse 1.
3. It was called the War of Camel because much of the fighting took place around the camel on which Ayesha was sitting to command her forces.
4. Margot Badran, *Feminists, Islam, and Nation*, p. 106.
5. John G. Stoessinger, "The Great Religions in Peace and War," in *Religious Humanism*, vol. xv, no. 3, Summer 1981.
6. *St. Louis Post-Dispatch*, August 12, 1993, p. 14A.
7. See Babylonian Talmud, Sanhedrin 108B; Genesis Rabbah 36:7; Ibn Qutayba (died 889), *Kitab al-ma'arif*; Ibn Hisham (died 828 or 833), *Kitab al-Tijan*; Ya'qubi (died 891-2), *Ta'rikh*. These sources are from the following papers presented at the annual meeting of the Middle East Studies Association, San Francisco, November 22-24, 1997: Benjamin Braude, "How Did Ham Become a Black Slave?: Reexamining the Noahides in the Abrahamic Tradition,"; Sidney H. Griffith, "Sons of Noah in Eastern Christian Tradition,"; Reuven Firestone, "The Sons of Noah in Sunni and Shiite Tafsir and Tradition,"; Gordon D. Newby, "Noah's Drowned Son." According to Ibn Qutayba "Ham b. Noah was a white man, handsome of face and form. God altered his color and the color of his progeny on account of prayer/curse (*da'wa*) of his father....They are the blacks....Ham begat Kush b. Ham and Kanaan and Fut b. Ham. As for Fut, he came to settle in the land of India. Its people are from his descendants. As for Cush and Canaan, the various types from Sudan, Nubia, al-Zanj, al-Zaghawa, Abyssinia, Copts, and Berbers come form his children." According to Ibn Hisham "Ham's wife gave birth to a black boy. He named him Kush and knew the prayer/curse (*al-da'wa*) had reached him."

GLOSSARY

Bakhtiar: Dr. Shahpour Bakhtiar was a leader in the INF. He was the only major political personality that foresaw the danger of Khomeini before the revolution. An old nemesis of the Shah, he agreed to assume prime ministership 37 days prior to the collapse of monarchy in order to prevent religious fascism. He was expelled from the INF for accepting prime ministership without permission from the INF. He was assassinated by agents of the fundamentalist regime in Paris on August 6, 1991.

Bani Sadr: He is a liberal Islamist. Became the first elected President of Iran in January 1980. Resisted Khomeini's moves to impose extremist dictatorship. Bani Sadr lost the power struggle to Khomeini and fundamentalists in the coup of June 1981.

Bazargan: Mehdi Bazargan founded the main liberal Islamist party in Iran called Nehzat Azadi Iran, translated as "Liberation Movement of Iran" or "Freedom Movement of Iran." He formed the provisional government after the collapse of monarchy in February 11, 1979. He resigned in protest when fundamentalists took over the US Embassy on November 4, 1979.

chador: Farsi term referring to an all-encompassing shapeless cloth for women that covers head to toe and only leaves face and hands uncovered.

Fadaian: Sazeman Cherik-hay Fadai Khalq Iran. It was created in the early 1960s. It was a Marxist-Leninist guerrilla organization. After the revolution, it split into numerous groups, the main two became known as Aghaliyat (Minority) and Aksariyat (Majority). Aghaliyat believed that the main contradiction was between capital and labor and that Iran was ready for a proletarian communist revolution: Aghaliyat opposed both the liberal democrats (as the base for bourgeoisie and imperialism) and Khomeini (as petty bourgeoisie). Aksariyat believed that the main contradiction was between imperialism (US) and the anti-imperialism (lead by Khomeini); therefore, Aksariyat supported Khomeini until it was violently repressed by Khomeini in 1983. In the 1997-present period, Aghaliyat continues to assume that a proletarian communist revolution is around the corner. Fadaian were very large and popular in 1979-1983. However, since the late 1980s, they have become very marginal in Iranian politics to the point of irrelevance.

fatwa: a religious decree issued by a high ranking Muslim cleric.

hejab: Islamic term meaning the covering for women.

Hezb Kommonist Kargari (HKK): Workers' Communist Party. The most extremist communist party in Iran. HKK regards the other communists, including all the former communist countries (and USSR since 1927) to be "bourgeois communists."

Hezbollah: Literary means the Party of God. It was the general term that fundamentalists used to refer to the extremist fundamentalist para-military thugs who terrorized the people after the rise of Khomeini to power. In the 1990s, the specific term "Ansar-e Hezbollah" was used for these para-military groups.

Iran National Front (INF): It was founded in 1949. It is the largest and oldest pro-democracy organization in Iran. It is a coalition of several groups, the largest being liberal democratic and social democratic. The INF advocates civil liberties, multiparty democracy, non-aligned foreign policy, non-violence, mixed-economy, juridical equality for men and women, and separation of religion and state.

Islamic Republican Party (IRP): Was established in 1979 after the revolution by the clerical supporters of Khomeini. It was the main fundamentalist party advocating a totalitarian rule by fundamentalist clerics. Opposed freedom and democracy as Western concepts alien to Islam. Strongly misogynist and violent. It organized the Pasdaran and Hezbollah to violently repress the people.

Liberation Movement of Iran (LMI): Also called Freedom Movement of Iran. It was founded in 1961. It combines liberal democracy and Islam as its political ideology. Middle of the road politics.

Khamanehi: Ayatollah Ali Khamanehi. A member of the fundamentalist elites since the 1979 Revolution. Earlier, he was identified with the "statist wing" of the fundamentalist elites; however, from 1989 when he replaced Rohollah Khomeini as the Supreme Leader, Khamanehi has embraced the "bazaari wing" of the fundamentalist elites.

Khatami: Hojatolislam Mohammad Khatami. A member of the "statist wing" of the fundamentalist elites since the 1979 Revolution. The Shoray Negahban allowed him to run for the Presidency in 1997. In the Presidential elections of May 1997, he ran as a reformist candidate and promoted a reduction of repression. He received 69% of the votes, although the Supreme Leader Ali Khamanehi had supported the rival candidate. Khatami was reelected in May 2001 for a second term.

Khomeini: Ayatollah Rohollah Khomeini. Supported the Shah and monarchy until 1959-1960 when due to the land reform and female franchise started opposing the Shah. Was a minor figure in the opposition until late 1977. By mid-1978 emerged as the leader of the revolution against the Shah by promising freedom, democracy and inchoate Islamic reforms to achieve social justice. Although the most powerful person in Iran from February 1979, he had to share power with non-fundamentalists until June 1981.

Kurdish Democratic Party of Iran (KDP-I): Prior to the revolution it was considered a conventional pro-Moscow communist party. In the post-revolutionary period, under the able leadership of Dr. Abdo-Rahman Ghassemlou, it became independent of Moscow. Unlike the Tudeh and the USSR it opposed Khomeini. The KDP-I was close to the Euro-Communist parties in 1979; however, it gradually embraced democratic socialism and joined the Socialist International. The KDP-I called for "autonomy for Kurdistan and democracy for Iran" in the post-revolutionary period. It joined the NCR in 1982 and left the coalition in the mid-1980s after the PMOI became authoritarian. Dr. Ghassemlou and two of his lieutenants were assassinated by agents of the fundamentalist government in Vienna on July 13, 1989. His successor, the new Secretary-General of the KDP-I, Dr. Sadegh Sharafkandi, along with two of his lieutenants and another leftist (former member of the ULC) were assassinated by the agents of the fundamentalist government on September 17, 1992, in Berlin. After the PMOI, the KDP-I was the largest armed resistance group in Iran. The KDP-I was able to mobilize the Kurdish peasantry as well as large sectors of the Kurdish intelligentsia.

Majles: A term used in Iran to refer to parliamentary assembly. The formal name was Majles Shoray Melli [National Consultative Assembly] which was created after the 1905-1906 Constitutional Revolution. After the fundamentalist took over in 1979, the name was changed to Majles Shoray Islami [Islamic Consultative Assembly].

Mossadegh: Dr. Mossadegh was the founder and leader of the INF. His government was overthrown by the CIA coup in August 1953. He is regarded as Iran's main democratic statesman. See Iran National Front.

National Council of Resistance: Created by the PMOI and President Bani Sadr in 1981 which attracted many progressive and liberal groups to it. By 1985-1986 almost all the members of the NCR had left the organization because of Rajavi's dictatorship. From then on, the NCR included PMOI and only a handful of individuals. Also see PMOI.

National Democratic Front (NDF): A democratic socialist organization, NDF was established by Dr. Hedayat Matin-Daftari (Mossadegh's grandson) and several Marxist intellectuals immediately after the revolution. It regarded the major contradiction to be between democracy and dictatorship. Its main goal was to create a broad-based coalition of leftist and centrist groups against what it called the right-wing fundamentalist "religious fascists." It was the first political group declared illegal by Khomeini. The NDF defended democratic rights of women, ethnic minorities and the press from fundamentalist attacks. It joined the NCR in 1981. It left the NCR in 1997 giving the reason as the PMOI's dictatorship.

Pasdaran: Short for Sepah Pasdaran Enghelab Islami. Refers to the formal fundamentalist military units established after the 1979 revolution to protect Khomeini's regime and suppress the opposition.

Paykar: or Peykar. See PMOI. The majority of the leaders of the PMOI in 1975 abandoned Islam and embraced Maoism as their ideology. However, they continued to keep the name PMOI until early 1979 when they took the name "Paykar." Paykar was very large in 1979-1981 period. It was the most radical of all the major communist groups. It condemned both liberal democrats and the fundamentalists as supporters of capitalism. It called for an immediate proletarian communist revolution. Paykar was Maoist (very Stalinist) organization. Within a few months after the June 1981 coup by the fundamentalists against Bani Sadr, the fundamentalists executed thousands of Paykar members and the organization totally disintegrated.

PMOI: Other acronyms include MKO (Mojahedin Khalq Organization), MEK (Mojahedin e Khalq). Also referred to as "Mojahedin" or "Iranian Mojahedin." It was founded in 1965 from a split from LMI. Its ideology was called Jame'e Bi-Tabagheh Towhidi [Divine Classless Society], which combined a Maoist version of communism with Islam. The founders were inspired by the success of the Chinese, Cuban and Algerian revolutions against Western colonial powers as well as the ongoing Vietnamese and Palestinians armed struggles. They adopted urban armed guerrilla strategy which consisted of assassinations of high officials of the Shah and his American advisors. In 1975, most of the leaders of the PMOI abandoned Islam and embraced Marxism-Leninism (Maoist variety). A small minority under the leadership of Masoud Rajavi remained Islamic (and communist). In the February 1979 to late 1980, their analysis was that the main contradiction in Iranian society was between imperialism and anti-imperialism. They sided with Khomeini (as leader of the anti-imperialist camp) and opposed the liberal democrats (whom they regarded to be representing the comprador bourgeoisie and paving the way for US imperialism). In late 1980, the PMOI changed its policy and started supporting Bani Sadr and opposing Khomeini. In 1981, the PMOI created the National Council of Resistance with President Bani Sadr and several other organizations. By 1985, almost all the members of the NCR had left the coalition due to Rajavi's terrible megalomania and dictatorship. The PMOI was the largest armed opposition group in the 1980s. The fundamentalist regime ruthlessly decimated their membership, executing about 20,000 of their members including raping large number of their female members before execution. In 1985-1986, PMOI leader, Mr. Rajavi transformed the PMOI into a totalitarian cult that would worship him. The PMOI had attracted a huge number of women to its rank and did pursue a policy of defending women's equality with men. The PMOI lost much of its popularity after its collaboration with Saddam Hussein in the middle of Iran-Iraq war. Many regard the PMOI to have become Iran's Khmer Rouge. Most Iranians regard the PMOI and its leader Masoud Rajavi to be subservient to Saddam Hussein.

Shah: Farsi term meaning "king." In this book, the term, "the Shah" refers to Mohammad Reza Pahlavi, who was the last Pahlavi monarch overthrown in 1979.

Shoray Maslehat Nezam: The Council for the Expediency of the System. It was created in 1989. There had been many conflicts between Majles and the Shorayeh Negahban and their conflicts were referred to Ayatollah Khomeini to resolve. Khomeini was ill most of the time and after his death, it was decided to create this institution to resolve the conflicts between Majles and Shoray Negahban. Its members are appointed by the Supreme Leader.

Shoray Negahban: The Council of Guardians. It was created by the fundamentalists after 1979 revolution. It has 12 members and its role was initially to vet all legislation passed by the Majles. Later on, it took the role of screening all candidates for Majles and Presidential elections, in effect banning anyone who was not a fundamentalist from running in the elections. It also bans fundamentalists that the members do not like from running in elections.

Sigheh: Sigheh is the Farsi word for the Arabic term "muta" or "mutah." It means "temporary marriage." It is when for a sum of money, a man and woman could contract a marriage for 1 hour to 99 years.

Tudeh: Tudeh Party is Iran's conventional pro-Moscow Communist Party (until the collapse of the USSR). It was the most organized party in Iran in the 1940s and 1950s. Due to its subservience to the USSR, it lost much of its appeal in the early 1960s. It supported Khomeini from February 1979 until it was repressed by Khomeini in 1983. It has been very marginal ever since to the point of irrelevance.

Ulama: Muslim clergy. Usually refers to those who are mid-ranking to high ranking clerics.

United Left Council for Democracy and Independence (ULC): Shoray Motahed Chap baray Democracy va Esteghlal. A small democratic socialist Marxian party, which was Iran's only socialist feminist organization in the 1981-1988 period. It dissolved sometimes in 1988. It joined the NCR. In 1985 after the transformation of the PMOI into a cult and the terrible dictatorship of Rajavi in NCR, the ULC left the NCR.

Velayat Faqih: The rule of the high ranking cleric. This doctrine was popularized by Ayatollah Rohollah Khomeini and enshrined in the fundamentalist constitution in Iran in 1979. The person who occupies this position is called Vali Faqih, or Supreme Leader.

SELECTED BIBLIOGRAPHY

Abrahamian, Ervand. *Iran Between Two Revolutions*. Princeton: Princeton University Press, 1982.

_____. *The Iranian Mojahedin*. New Haven and London: Yale University Press, 1989.

Afari, Janet. "On the Origins of Feminism in Early 20th-Century Iran." *Journal of Women's History* 1, no. 2 (Fall 1989): 65-87.

Afshar, Haleh, ed. *Iran: A Revolution in Turmoil*. Albany: State University of New York Press, 1985.

_____. "Women, State and Ideology in Iran." *Third World Quarterly* 7, no. 2 (April 1985): 256-278.

_____, ed. *Women, State, and Ideology: Studies from Africa and Asia*. Albany: State University of New York Press, 1987.

Agha Haji Mirza Mahdi Pooya Yazdi, Ayatollah. "Special Notes...On the Philosophic Aspects of some of the Verses." In *The Holy Qur'an*, translated by S. V. Mir Ahmed Ali. 2nd ed. Elmhurst, NY: Tahrike Tarsile Qur'an, Inc., 1995.

Ahmed, Leila. "Early Islam and the Position of Women: The Problem of Interpretation." In *Wemen in Middle Eastern Histories: Shifting Boundaries in Sex and Gender*, eds. Nikki Keddie and Beth Baron, 58-73. New Haven and London: Yale University Press, 1991.

_____. *Women and Gender In Islam: Historical Roots of a Modern Debate*. New Haven and London: Yale University Press, 1992.

Akhavi, Shahrough. "Clerical Politics in Iran Since 1979." In *The Iranian Revolution and the Islamic Republic*, eds. Nikki Keddie and Eric Hooglund, 57-73. Syracuse: Syracuse University Press, 1986.

Albert, Michael et al., *Liberating Theory*. Boston: South End Press, 1986.

Amnesty International. *Evidence of Torture in Iran*. AI Index: MDE 13/03/84. August 1984.

_____. *Iran Briefing*. AI Index: MDE 13/08/87. August 1987.

_____. *Human Rights Violations against Shi'a Religious Leaders and their Followers*. June 1997.

Andersen, Margaret L. *Thinking About Women: Sociological Perspectives on Sex and Gender*. 2nd edition. New York: Macmillan Publishing Company, 1988.

Andersen, Margaret L., and Patricia Hill Collins, eds. *Race, Class, and Gender: An Anthology*. Belmont, CA: Wadsworth Publishing Company, 1992.

Andersen, Roy R., Robert F. Seibert and Jon G. Wagner, *Politics and Change in the Middle East: Sources of Conflict and Accommodation*. 3rd ed. Englewood Cliffs, NJ: Prentice Hall, 1990.

Arjomand, Said Amir. *The Turban for the Crown: The Islamic Revolution in Iran*. New York: Oxford University Press, 1988.

Avineri, Shlomo. *The Social & Political Thought of Karl Marx*. Cambridge: Cambridge University Press, 1968, 1980.

Ayubi, Nazih N. "Rethinking the Public/Private Dichotomy: Radical Islamism and Civil Society in the Middle East." *Contention: Debates in Society, Culture, and Sciences* 4, no. 3 (Spring 1995): 79-105.

Az. "The Women's Struggle in Iran." *Monthly Review* 32, no. 10 (March 1981): 22-30.

Azari, Farah, ed. *Women of Iran: The Conflict with Fundamentalist Islam*. London: Ithaca Press, 1983.

Bakhash, Shaul. *The Reign of the Ayatollahs: Iran and the Islamic Revolution*. New York: Basic Books, 1984.

Bani-Sadr, Abol Hassan. *Barnameh Hokomat Jomhori Islami*. [Program of the Government of the Islamic Republic]. n.p. n.d.

_____. *Khianat Be Omid*. [Treason to Hope]. n.p. n.d.

_____. "I Defeated the Ideology of the Regime." Interview by Fred Halliday (Paris, France, August 1981). *MERIP Reports*, no. 104 (March-April 1982): 5-8.

_____. *My Turn to Speak: Iran, the Revolution & Secret Deals with the U.S.*. From a series of interviews by Jean-Charles Deniau. Washington: Brassey's Inc., a Macmillan Publishing Company, 1991.

Banuazizi, Ali, and Myron Weiner, eds. *The State, Religion, and Ethnic Politics: Afghanistan, Iran, and Pakistan*. Syracuse: Syracuse University Press, 1986.

Banuazizi, Ali. "Social-Psychological Approaches to Political Development." In *Understanding Political Development*, eds., Myron Weiner and Samuel Huntington.

Bauer, Janet. "Iranian Women: How Many Faces Behind the Veil?" *East-West Perspectives: Journal of the East-West Center* 1, no. 4 (Fall 1980): 21-25.

_____. "Poor Women and Social Consciousness in Revolutionary Iran." In *Women and Revolution in Iran*, ed. Guity Nashat, 141-169. Boulder, CO: Westview Press, 1983.

_____. "Demographic Change, Women and the Family in a Migrant Neighborhood of Tehran." In *Women and the Family in Iran*, ed. Asghar Fathi, 158-186. Netherlands: E. J. Brill, 1985.

Bazargan, Mehdi. *Enghelab Iran Dar Do Harakat* [Iranian Revolution in Two Moves]. Tehran: Mazaheri, 1984.

Beck, Lois, and Nikki Keddie, eds. *Women in the Muslim World*. Cambridge: Harvard University Press, 1978.

Benard, Cheryl. "Islam and Women: Some Reflections on the Experience of Iran." *Journal of South Asian and Middle Eastern Studies* IV, no. 2 (Winter 1980): 10-26.

Bonine, Michael, and Nikki Keddie, eds. *Modern Iran: The Dialectics of Continuity and Change*. Albany: State University New York Press, 1981.

Chehabi, H. E. *Iranian Politics and Religious Modernism: The Liberation Movement of Iran Under the Shah and Khomeini*. Ithaca and New York: Cornell University Press, 1990.

Cole, Juan R. I., and Nikki Keddie, eds. *Shi'ism and Social Protest*. New Haven and London: Yale University Press, 1986.

Congressional Quarterly. *The Middle East*. Seventh edition. Washington, D.C.: Congressional Quarterly, 1991.

Daly, Mary. *Gyn/Ecology: the Metaethics of Radical Feminism*. Boston: Beacon Press, 1978.

Dashti, 'Ali. *Twenty Three Years: A Study of the Prophetic Career of Mohammad*. Translated from the Persian by F. R. C. Bagley. Costa Mesa, CA: Mazda Publishers, 1994.

Dill, Bonnie Thornthon. "Race, Class, and Gender: Prospects for an All-Inclusive Sisterhood." *Feminist Studies* 9, no. 1 (Spring 1983): 131-150.

Di Stefano, Christine. "Who the Heck are We? The Theoretical Turn Against Gender." Paper prepared for delivery at the 1990 Annual Meeting of the Western Political Science Association, Newport Beach, California, March 22-24, 1990.

Draper, Hal. *Karl Marx's Theory of Revolution*. vol. 1, *State and Bureaucracy*. New York: Monthly Review Press, 1977.

Echols, Alice. "The New Feminism of Yin and Yang." In *Powers of Desire: The Politics of Sexuality*, eds. Ann Snitow, Christine Stansell and Sharon Thompson, 439-459. New York: Monthly Review Press, 1983.

Eisenstein, Zillah R., ed. *Capitalist Patriarchy and the Case for Socialist Feminism*. New York: Monthly Review Press, 1979.

_____. *Feminism and Sexual Equality: Crisis in Liberal America*. New York: Monthly Review Press, 1984.

Enayat, Hamid. *Modern Islamic Political Thought*. Austin, TX: University of Texas Press, 1982.

Engels, Friedrich. *The Origins of the Family, Private Property and the State*. Introduction by Michele Barrett. New York: Penguin Books, 1985, [original 1884].

Esposito, John L. "Introduction: Women in Islam and Muslim Societies." In *Islam, Gender, and Social Change*, eds. Yvonne Yazbeck Haddad and John L. Esposito, ix-xxviii. New York and Oxford: Oxford University Press, 1998.

Esposito, John L. et al., eds. *The Oxford Encyclopedia of the Modern Islamic World*. Four Volumes. New York and Oxford: Oxford University Press, 1995.

Fallaci, Oriana. "Mohammed Riza Pahlavi." Chap. in *Interview With History*. 262-287. Boston: Houghton Mifflin Company, 1976.

_____. "An Interview with Khomeini." *New York Times Magazine*, October 7, 1979, 29.

_____. "'Everybody Wants to be Boss': An Interview with Mehdi Bazargan, Prime Minister of Iran." *New York Times Magazine*, October 28, 1979, 20.

Faludi, Susan. "Backlash." In *Feminism in Our Time: The Essential Writings, World War II to the Present*, edited and with an introduction and commentaries by Miriam Schneir, 454-468. New York: Vintage Books, 1994.

Fathi, Asghar, ed. *Women and the Family in Iran*. Netherlands: E. J. Brill, 1985.

Feldberg, Roslyn L. "Women, Self-Management, and Socialism." *Socialist Review*, no. 56 (1981): 141-152.

Ferdows, Adele K. "Women and the Islamic Revolution." *International Journal of Middle East Studies* 15, no. 2 (May 1983): 283-298.

Ferdows, Amir H. "Khomaini and Fadayan's Society and Politics." *International Journal of Middle East Studies* 15, no. 2 (May 1983): 241-257.

Firestone, Shulamith. *The Dialectic of Sex: The Case for Feminist Revolution*. New York: William Morrow, 1970.

Floor, Willem. "The Revolutionary Character of Iranian Ulama: Wishful Thinking or Reality?" *International Journal of Middle East Studies* 12, no. 1 (December 1980): 501-524.

Friedl, Erika. "State Ideology and Village Women." In *Women and Revolution in Iran*, ed., Nashat.

Frye, Marilyn. *The Politics of Reality: Essays in Feminist Theory*. Trumansburg, NY: Crossing Press, 1983.

Gasiorowski, Mark J. "The 1953 Coup d'Etat in Iran." *International Journal of Middle East Studies* 19, no. 3 (August 1987): 261-286.

Ghahreman, Sahar. "The Islamic Government Policy Towards Women's Access to Higher Education in Iran." *Nimeye Digar: Persian Language Feminist Journal*, no. 7 (Summer 1988): 16-29.

Gilligan, Carol. *In a Different Voice: Psychological Theory and Women's Development*. Cambridge, MA: Harvard University Press, 1982.

Glossop, Ronald, *Confronting War: An Examination of Humanity's Most Pressing Problem*, 2 ed. Jefferson, North Carolina: McFarland & Company, Inc., Publishers, 1987.

Haeri, Shahla. "Temporary Marriage and the State in Iran: An Islamic Discourse on Female Sexuality." *Social Research* 59, no. 1 (Spring 1992): 201-223.

Hajj Sayyed Javadi, Ali Asghar. *Az Sedaye Paye Fashism ta Ghoole Fashism ke dar Hale Tassalot Bar Sarasar-e Iran Ast*. [From Warning of Early Steps of Fascism to Fascist Specter That is in the Process of Dominating the Entire Iran]. Tehran: n.p. n.d. reprint in Berlin,

Germany: Koshesh Barayeh Pishbord Nehzat Melli Iran Publishers, Esfand 1359/1980.

Hartmann, Heidi. "Capitalism, Patriarchy, and Job Segregation by Sex." *Signs: Journal of Women in Culture and Society* 1, no. 3, part 2 (Spring 1976): 137-169.

_____. "The Unhappy Marriage of Marxism and Feminism: Towards a More Progressive Union." In *Women and Revolution: A Discussion of the Unhappy Marriage of Marxism and Feminism*, ed. Lydia Sargent, 1-41. Boston: South End Press, 1981.

Hatem, Mervat. "Class and Patriarchy as Competing Paradigms for the Study of Middle Eastern Women." *Comparative Studies in Society and History* 29, no. 4 (October 1987): 811-818.

Hegland, Mary Elaine. "'Traditional' Iranian Women: How They Cope." *The Middle East Journal* 36, no. 4 (Autumn 1982): 483-501.

_____. "Political Roles of Iranian Village Women." *MERIP Middle East Report*, no. 138 (January-February 1986): 14-46.

Al-Hibri, Azizah. "A Study of Islamic Herstory: Or How Did We Ever Get Into This Mess?." *Women's Studies International Forum* 5, no. 2 (1982): 207-219.

Higgins, Patricia. "Women in the Islamic Republic of Iran: Legal, Social, and Ideological Changes." *Signs: Journal of Women in Culture and Society* 10, no. 3 (Spring 1985): 477-494.

Himmelweit, Susan. "The Real Dualism of Sex and Class." *Review of Radical Political Economics* 16, no. 1 (Spring 1984): 167-183.

Hoodfar, Homa. "Devices and Desires: Population Policy and Gender Roles in the Islamic Republic." *MERIP Middle East Report*, no. 190 (September-October 1994): 11-17.

Ibrahim, Mahmood. *Merchant Capital and Islam*. Austin: University of Texas Press, 1990.

Irfani, Suroosh. *Iran's Islamic Revolution: Popular Liberation or Religious Dictatorship?*. London: Zed Books, Ltd., 1983.

Islamic Republic of Iran, Plan and Budget Organization, Statistical Centre of Iran. *Sarshomari Omomi Nofus va Maskan Mehr 1365: Natayj-e Nahaii*. [Census 1986: Final Results]. In Farsi. Tehran: Statistical Centre of Iran Press, 1989.

_____. *Iran Statistical Yearbook: 1369 [March 1990-March 1991]*. In Farsi. Tehran: Statistical Centre of Iran Press, 1992.

Jagger, Alison M., and Paula S. Rothenberg, eds. *Feminist Frameworks: Alternative Theoretical Accounts of the Relations Between Women and Men*, 2nd edition, New York: McGraw-Hill, 1984

JAMI. *Gozashteh Cheragh Rah Ayandeh Ast: Tarikh Iran dar Fasele Do Kodeta 1299-1332*. [Past is the Illumination of Future: Iran's History Between the two Coup d'etats 1921-1953]. 2nd edition. Tehran: Ghoghnoos Publishers, 1367/1989.

Kandiyoti, Deniz, ed. *Women, Islam and the State*. Philadelphia: Temple University Press, 1991.

Kavian, Amir. *Mardi Ke Az Tarikh Amad*. 2nd edition. Tehran: Entesharat Kalk Khiyal, 1378.

Kazemi, Farhad. "The *Fada'iyan-e Islam*: Fanaticism, Politics and Terror." In *From Nationalism to Revolutionary Islam*, ed. Said Amir Arjomand, 158-176. Albany: State University of New York Press, 1984.

Kazemzadeh, Masoud. "Teaching the Politics of Islamic Fundamentalism." *PS: Political Science and Politics* 31, 1 (March 1998).

Keddie, Nikki. "Problems in the Study of Middle Eastern Women." *International Journal of Middle East Studies* 10, no. 2 (May 1979): 225-240.

_____. "Introduction: Deciphering Middle Eastern Women's History," in *Women in Middle Eastern History: Shifting Boundaries in Sex and Gender*, eds., Nikki Keddie and Beth Baron, 1-22. New Haven and London: Yale University Press, 1991.

Keddie, Nikki, and Eric Hooglund, eds. *The Iranian Revolution and the Islamic Republic*. Revised edition. Syracuse: Syracuse University Press, 1986.

Kelber, Kim. "Iran: Five Days in March." *MS.*, June 1979, 90.

Khalili, Mohammad Ali. *Zendegani Hazrat Ali Alayhe Salaam Amir al-Momenin*. 2nd edition. Tehran: Eqbal Publishers, 1377 [1998].

Khalilullah Moghadam, Ahmad. *Mobarezeh Ba Fashim-e Mazhabi*. [Struggle Against Religious Fascism]. Organized by Mohammad Biglari. Encino, CA: Ketab Corp., n.d.

Khalkhali, Sadegh. "All the People Who Are Opposed to Our Revolution Must Die." Interviewer not identified (Summer 1980). *MERIP Reports*, no. 104 (March-April 1982): 30-31.

Khomeini, Ruhollah. *Tozih al-Masael: Resaleh Amalieh Imam Khomeini*. [Explanation of Problems]. Kanon Entesharat Mehrab, n.d. [late 1980s edition].

_____. *Velayat Faghih: Hokomat Islami*. [Guardianship of the Jurisconsult: Islamic Government]. Tehran: Amir Kabir Press, 1979 edition. [originally delivered as lectures 1969-1970].

_____. "The Start of a Gigantic Explosion." an interview with *Le Monde* published in *MERIP Reports*, no. 69 (July-August 1978): 19-20.

_____. *Islam and Revolution: Writings and Declarations of Imam Khomeini*. Translated and annotated by Hamid Algar. Berkeley: Mizan Press, 1981. Reprint London: Routledge & Kegan Paul, 1981.

_____. "Payam-e Sarnevesht Saz va Besiar Mohem Hazrat Imam Modazeleh." *Pasdar Islam*, no. 88 (Farvardin 1368): 4-21.

_____. *Sahifeh Enghelab: Vasiyat Nameh Siasi-Elahi Rahbar Kabir Enghelab Islami va Bobyangozar Jomhuri Islami Iran*. [Political-Divine Will of Ayatollah Khomeini]. Tehran: Ministry of Culture and Islamic Guidance Publications, 1372/1992 edition. [first published 1989].

King, Deborah K. "Multiple Jeopardy, Multiple Consciousness: The Context of a Black Feminist Ideology." *Signs: Journal of Women in Culture and Society* 14, no. 1 (1988): 42-72.

Ladjevardi, Habib. "The Origins of U.S. Support for an Autocratic Iran." *International Journal of Middle East Studies* 15, no. 2 (May 1983): 225-239.

_____. *Labour Unions and Autocracy in Iran*. Syracuse: Syracuse University Press, 1985.

Lewis, Bernard. *The Middle East: A Brief History of the Last 2,000 Years*. New York: Scribner, 1995.

Lief, Louise, and Richard Z. Chesnoff. "Freeing Hostages, Hiring Hit Squads." *U.S. News & World Report*, October 7, 1991, 52.

MacKinnon, Catharine. "Feminism, Marxism, Method, and the State: An Agenda for Theory." In *Feminist Theory: A Critique of Ideology*, eds. Nannerl Keohane, Michelle Rosaldo and Barbara Gelpi, 1-30. Chicago: University of Chicago Press, 1982.

Mahdavi, Shireen. "Shawhar Ahu Khanum: Passion, Polygyny and Tragedy." *Middle Eastern Studies* 24, no. 1 (January 1988): 113-117.

_____. "The Position of Women in Shi'a Iran: Views of the 'Ulama." In *Women and the Family in the Middle East: New Voices of Change*, ed. 255-268. Elizabeth Fernea, Austin: University of Texas Press, 1985.

Marcuse, Herbert. "Socialist Feminism: The Hard Core of the Dream." *Edcentric*, nos. 31-32, November 1974, 7.

Marx, Karl. *Economic and Philosophical Manuscripts of 1844* in *Karl Marx: Early Writings*, ed., Quintin Hoare, 279-400. New York: Vintage Books, 1975.

Matin-Daftari, Hedayat. "Mossadeq's Legacy Today." Interview by Fred Halliday (London, late 1981 and summer 1982). *MERIP Reports*, no. 113 (March-April 1983): 24-25.

Maud, Constance Elizabeth. "The First Persian Feminist: Quarratu'l'ain." *The Fortnightly Review* 93 (June 1913): 1175-1182.

Mernissi, Fatima. *Beyond the Veil: Male-Female Dynamics in Modern Muslim Society*. 1975; revised ed. Bloomington and Indianapolis: Indiana University Press, 1987.

_____. "Virginity and Patriarchy." *Women's Studies International Forum* 5, no. 2 (1982): 183-191.

_____. *The Veil and the Male Elite: A Feminist Interpretation of Women's Rights in Islam*. 1987; Translated by Mary Jo Lakeland. Reading, Massachusetts: Addison-Wesley Publishing Company, 1991.

_____. "Muslim Women and Fundamentalism." *MERIP Middle East Report*, no. 153 (July-August 1988): 8-11.

Middle East Watch, *Iran: Arrests of "Loyal Opposition" Politicians*. New York: Human Rights Watch, June 29, 1990.

_____. *Iran: Political Dissidents, Held for Over a Year, Are Reportedly Sentenced*. New York: Human Rights Watch, September 3, 1991.

_____. *Guardians of Thought: Limits on Freedom of Expression in Iran*. New York: Human Rights Watch, August 1993.

Mill, John Stuart, and Harriet Taylor Mill, *Essays on Sex Equality*. Edited and with an introductory essay by Alice S. Rossi. Chicago: University of Chicago Press, 1970.

Moaddel, Mansoor. "Class Struggle in Post-Revolutionary Iran." *International Journal of Middle East Studies* 23, no. 3 (August 1991): 317-343.

_____. *Class, Politics, and Ideology in the Iranian Revolution*. New York: Columbia University Press, 1993.

Moghadam, Val. "Women, Work and Ideology in the Islamic Republic." *International Journal of Middle East Studies* 20, no. 2 (May 1988): 221-243.

_____. "Problems in Middle East Women's Studies: The View from Marxist-Feminist Sociology." Paper presented to the annual meeting of Middle East Studies Association, 1989.

_____. *Modernizing Women: Gender & Social Change in the Middle East.* Boulder and London: Lynne Rienner Publishers, 1993.

_____, ed. *Identity Politics and Women: Cultural Reassertions and Feminisms in International Perspective.* Boulder: Westview Press, 1994.

_____, ed. *Gender and National Identity: Women and Politics in Muslim Societies.* London and New Jersey: Zed Books, Ltd., 1994.

Mortimer, Edward. *Faith and Power: the Politics of Islam.* London: Faber & Faber, 1982.

Munson, Jr., Henry. *Islam and Revolution in the Middle East.* New Haven and London: Yale University Press, 1988.

Najmabadi, Afsaneh. "Iran's Turn to Islam: From Modernism to a Moral Order." *Middle East Journal* 41, no. 2 (Spring 1987): 202-217.

_____. "Fazayeh Tang Nasazegari: Zan Irani Dar Daheh Enghelab" [Any Space for Difference?: Iranian Women in the Decade of Revolution]. *Nimeye Digar: Persian Language Feminist Journal*, no. 11 (Spring 1990): 15-40.

_____. "Hazards of Modernity and Morality: Women, State and Ideology in Contemporary Iran." In *Women, Islam and the State*, ed. Deniz Kandiyoti, 48-76. Philadelphia: Temple University Press, 1991.

Nashat, Guity, ed. *Women and Revolution in Iran.* Boulder: Westview Press, 1983.

"The New Woman in Persia." *The Muslim World* 1, no. 2 (April 1911): 185-186. [no author].

Nima, Ramy. *The Wrath of Allah: Islamic Revolution and Reaction in Iran.* London: Pluto Press, 1983.

O'Reilly, Jane. "The Unfinished Revolution: For Iran's Women, the Real Struggle Goes on." In *Time Magazine*, April 2, 1979, 34.

Owen, Roger. *State, Power & Politics in the Making of the Modern Middle East.* London and New York: Routledge, 1992.

Paidar, Parvin. *Women and the Political Process in Twentieth-Century Iran.* Cambridge and New York: Cambridge University Press, 1995.

The People's Mojahedin Organization of Iran. *Erteja Chist? va Mortaje Kist?.* [What is Reaction? and Who is Reactionary?]. Tehran: Entesharat Sazeman Mojahedin Khalq Iran, Mordad 1359 [July 1980].

_____. *Mojahed.* in Farsi. various issues.

_____. *Mojahed.* in English. vol. 1, no. 5. (May 1980).

_____. *At War With Humanity...: A Report on the Human Rights Records of Khomeini's Regime.* France: May 1982.

_____. *Barnameh Dolat Movaghat Jomhuri Democratic Islami Iran*. [The Program of the Provisional Government of the Islamic Democratic Republic of Iran]. Long Beach, CA: Muslim Student Society, n.d. [circa 1981]

_____. *Barnameh Shorayh Melli Moghavemat va Dolat Movaghat Jomhori Democratic Islami Iran*. [The Program of the National Council of Resistance and the Provisional Government of the Islamic Democratic Republic of Iran]. Publication of Dabirkhaneh National Council of Resistance, Tir 30, 1363 [1984].

Peretz, Don. *The Middle East Today*. 5th edition. New York: Praeger, 1988.

Rahnema, Ali, and Farhad Nomani. *The Secular Miracle: Religion, Politics & Economic Policy in Iran*. London and New Jersey: Zed Books Ltd., 1990.

Ramazani, Nesta. "Behind the Veil: Status of Women in Revolutionary Iran." *Journal of South Asian and Middle Eastern Studies* IV, no. 2 (Winter 1980): 27-36.

_____. "Women in Iran: The Revolutionary Ebb and Flow." *Middle East Journal* 47, no. 3 (Summer 1993): 409-428.

Reeves, Minou. *Female Warriors of Allah: Women and the Islamic Revolution*. New York: E. P. Dutton, 1989.

Rezai, Behjat. "Mosaic: Out of the Frying Pan into the Fire." *The Middle East*, May 1991, 43.

Rich, Adrienne. *Of Women Born: Motherhood as Experience and Institution*. New York: W. W. Norton, 1976; reprint, Toronto and New York: Bantam Books, 1977.

Rothenberg, Paula S., ed. *Racism and Sexism: An Integrated Study*. New York: St. Martin's Press, 1988.

Rubin, Gayle. "The Traffic in Women: Notes on the 'Political Economy' of Sex." In *Toward an Anthropology of Women*, ed. Rayna R. Reiter, 157-210. New York: Monthly Review Press, 1975.

El Saadawi, Nawal. *The Hidden Face of Eve: Women in the Arab World*. Translated by Dr. Sherif Hetata. Zed Press, 1980; foreword by Irene Gendzier, reprint, Boston: Beacon Press, 1982.

_____. "Woman and Islam." *Women's Studies International Forum* 5, no. 2 (1982): 193-206.

Saeedian, Abdol Hussein. *Majmoay Az Adab va Rosoom Ezdevaj va Talagh Dar Manategh Mokhtalef Iran*. [A Collection of Customs and Rules Pertaining to Marriage and Divorce in Various Parts of Iran]. Compiled by the Independent Democratic Grouping of Iranian Women in Europe. Hannover, West Germany: n.p. n.d.

Sahabi, Engineer Ezatollah. "Tajrobehe Jomhori Islami Iran" [The Experience of the Islamic Republic of Iran]. *Ihya.* [Regeneration]. Tehran: n.p. n.d. 10-64.

Sanasarian, Eliz. *The Women's Rights Movement in Iran: Mutiny, Appeasement, & Repression from 1900 to Khomeini.* New York: Praeger, 1981.

_____. "Political Activism and Islamic Identity in Iran." In *Women in the World: 1975-1985 The Women's Decade,* eds. Lynne Iglitzin and Ruth Ross, 207-223. second revised ed. Santa Barbara and Oxford: ABC-CLIO, 1986.

_____. "The Politics of Gender and Development in the Islamic Republic of Iran." *Journal of Developing Societies* 8 (1992): 56-68.

_____. "An Analysis of Fida'i and Mujahidin Positions on Women's Rights." In *Women and Revolution in Iran,* ed., Guity Nashat.

Sancton, Thomas. "The Tehran Connection: An Exclusive Look at How Iran Hunts Down Its Opponents Abroad." *Time Magazine,* March 21, 1994, 50.

Schmidt, Steffen W. et al. *American Government and Politics Today: 1993-1994 Edition.* St. Paul: West Publishing Company, 1993.

Schneir, Miriam. ed. *Feminism: The Essential Historical Writings.* New York: Vintage Books, 1972.

Shahidian, Hammed. "The Iranian Left and the 'Woman Question' in the Revolution of 1978-79." *International Journal of Middle East Studies* 26, no. 2 (May 1994): 223-247.

Shariati, Ali. *Aree Inchenin Bood Aye Bradar.* [Yes, It Was Like That Brother]. n.p. n.d.

_____. *Fatima Fatima Ast.* [Fatima is Fatima]. n.p. n.d.

Shepard, William E. "Islam and Ideology: Towards A Typology." *International Journal of Middle East Studies* 19, no. 3 (August 1987): 307-336.

Shoaee, Rokhsareh. "The Mujahid Women of Iran: Reconciling 'Culture' and 'Gender'." *Middle East Journal* 41, no. 4 (Autumn 1987): 519-537.

Shuster, W. Morgan. *The Strangling of Persia.* New York: The Century Co., 1912.

Simons, Margaret A. "Beauvoir and the Roots of Radical Feminism." Unpublished paper. 1992 draft.

Smith, Jane I., and Yvonne Y. Haddad, "Eve: Islamic Image of Woman." *Women's Studies International Forum* 5, no. 2 (1982): 135-144.

Stack, Carol B. "The Culture of Gender: Women and Men of Color." *Signs: Journal of Women in Culture and Society* (Winter 1986): 321-324.

Stocking, Annie Woodman. "The New Woman In Persia." *The Muslim World* 2, no. 4 (October 1912): 367-371.

Stoessinger, John G. "The Great Religions in Peace and War." *Religious Humanism* XV, no. 3 (Summer 1981): 108-113.

Swerdlow, Amy, and Hanna Lessinger, eds. *Class, Race, and Sex: The Dynamics of Control*. Boston: G. K. Hall & Co., 1983.

Tabari, Azar [psued. of Afsaneh Najmabadi]. "The Enigma of Veiled Iranian Women." *Feminist Review*, no. 5 (1980). Reprint New York: Women's International Resource Exchange.

_____. "The Rise of Islam: What Did Happen to Women?" *Khamsin: Journal of Revolutionary Socialists of the Middle East*, no. 10 (1983). Reprint New York: Women's International Resource Exchange.

_____. "Chronology." *Nimeye Digar: Persian Language Feminist Quarterly*, no. 2 (Autumn 1984): 126-134.

_____. "The Women's Movement in Iran: A Hopeful Prognosis." *Feminist Studies* 12, no. 2 (Summer 1986): 343-360.

Tabari, Azar, and Nahid Yeganeh, eds. *In the Shadow of Islam: The Women's Movement in Iran*. London: Zed Press, 1982.

Tohidi, Nayereh. *Zan va Gheshriyoun Islami*. [Women and Fundamentalism in Contemporary Iran]. Los Angeles: n.p. 1988.

Tong, Rosemarie. *Feminist Thought: A Comprehensive Introduction*. Boulder, CO: Westview Press, 1989.

Touba, Jacquiline Rudolph. "Sex Segregation and Women's Roles in the Economic System: The Case of Iran." In *Research in the Interweave of Social Roles: Women and Men*, ed. Helena Z. Lopata, 51-98. Greenwich, Conn.: JAI Press, 1980.

Toubia, Nahid, ed. *Women of the Arab World*. London: Zed Books, 1988.

Tucker, Judith. "Problems in the Historiography of Women in the Middle East." *International Journal of Middle East Studies* 15, no. 3 (August 1983): 321-336.

U.S. Government. American University. *Iran: A Country Study-Area Handbook Series 1978*. Washington, D.C.: GPO, 1978.

U.S. Government. Department of the Army. *Iran: A Country Study-Area Handbook Series 1989*. Washington, D.C.: GPO, 1989.

Vatandoust, Gholam-Reza. "The Status of Iranian Women During the Pahlavi Regime." In *Women and the Family in Iran*, ed., Asghar Fathi.

Weiner, Myron, and Samuel P. Huntington, eds. *Understanding Political Development*. Boston: Little, Brown and Company, 1987.

Wiley, Joyce N. "Kho'i, Abol-Qasem." In *The Oxford Encyclopedia of the Modern Islamic World*, ed., John L. Esposito.

Winsor, Mary. "The Blossoming of a Persian Feminist." *Equal Rights* (Washington: National Women's Party), October 23, 1926, 293.

Woolf, Virginia. *Three Guineas*. New York: Harcourt Brace, 1938.

Yeganeh, Nahid. "The Women's Movement in Iran." *Nimeye Digar: Persian Language Feminist Quarterly*, no. 2 (Autumn 1984): 7-28.

Zein Ed-Din, Nazirah. "Removing the Veil and Veiling: Lectures and Reflections Towards Women's Liberation and Social Reform in the Islamic World." *Women's Studies International Forum* 5, no. 2 (1982): 221-226. Translated by Salah-Dine Hammoud.

ABOUT THE AUTHOR

M asoud Kazemzadeh, Ph.D. is Assistant Professor in the Depart-
ment of Political Science at Utah Valley State College. He
received B.S. in International Relations from the University of Minnesota,
and M.A. and Ph.D. in Political Science from the University of Southern
California. He was a post-doctoral fellow at the Center for Middle Eastern
Studies at Harvard University in 1998. He is the recipient of the Western
Political Science Association's "Best Dissertation in Political Science
Award" for 1996. He also received an Honorable Mention from the
Foundation for Iranian Studies for the "Best Dissertation of the Year on a
Topic of Iranian Studies" (1996). His articles have been published in *PS:
Political Science and Politics*, *Middle East Policy*, *Comparative Studies of
South Asia, Africa and the Middle East*, *St. Louis Post-Dispatch*, and *The
Salt Lake Tribune*. He is also the author of *Marxism, Leninism, and Social
Democracy: Ideological Premises of Dictatorship and Democracy* (Los
Angeles: Arta Books, 2001). Dr. Kazemzadeh is a member of Iran National
Front.